DYNAMITE
AND
PEACE

by Edith Patterson Meyer

Scientist, inventor, champion of peace — Alfred Nobel was a man seemingly of strange contradictions; a man certainly far ahead of his time. He made millions through the invention and sale of high explosives; with those millions he endowed the prizes that bear his name — prizes for science, for literature, and for peace.

Though the name of Alfred Nobel is famous in connection with those prizes, most people know very little about this remarkable man. In this very human and dramatic biography he emerges — the tireless inventor with the business brain, the optimist who thought the awful power of dynamite would discourage wars, the realist who could change his views if progress toward peace required it.

Nobel was farsighted in science and also in the ways of the world. He was a pioneer in the development of synthetics made from cellulose. His internationalism seems more of today than of yesterday. For young men and women of the present his life and his actions, as recounted in this book, offer fascinating food for thought.

Jacket and frontispiece by
Leonard Everett Fisher

DYNAMITE AND PEACE

The Story of Alfred Nobel

DYNAMITE
AND
PEACE

by *Edith Patterson Meyer*

LITTLE, BROWN and COMPANY
Boston · Toronto

Published simultaneously in Canada
by Little, Brown & Company (Canada) Limited

PRINTED IN THE UNITED STATES OF AMERICA

Contents

To my brothers

Walter · Herbert · Robert

Dynamite and Peace

I

Childhood

in

Sweden

"ALFRED says he's going to school. Is he, Mother?" Robert burst into the little kitchen and flung the question at his mother eagerly.

Fru Nobel nodded, then calmly went on peeling the big panful of potatoes. "You started when you were eight; Ludwig started when he was eight. Alfred will be eight in October. You don't think he should stay home this first month of school just waiting for his birthday, do you?" She smiled up at her oldest son, her paring knife poised in mid-air.

Robert hesitated. "No, of course not. But Alfred is different from Ludwig and me. He's sickly. You said so yourself. He never goes out to play with the other boys. He's always lying down."

"The more reason for him to go to school," Fru Nobel said firmly. "It will do him good. Robert" — she looked directly into her son's eyes — "you are twelve and Ludwig is ten. I shall depend on you both to see that your brother gets to and from school safely. In school, he is well able to look after himself."

Robert knew that this was so. When it was talk, not play, Alfred could hold his own with any of them. He met his mother's look and nodded.

Alfred was standing in the doorway. He had overheard part of the conversation from the couch in the combination living-dining room. "I can go, can't I, Mother? I want to go so much!" The blue eyes in the thin face were full of longing.

"Yes," his mother told him, "you can go. But you must eat more and try your best to get strong and well."

"I will," Alfred promised happily. "Oh, I will!"

Robert went out to deliver another order for the grocer on the corner. Alfred drew up a chair beside his mother. From Ludwig's old reader he spelled out

4

words and with her help succeeded in reading a few lines.

"Close the book now and set the table for me," Fru Nobel said when the potatoes were peeled and the meatballs mixed.

Soon Robert and Ludwig came in together, letting into the little house a great gust of the crisp Stockholm early autumn air.

"You must have smelled the dinner!" Their mother laughed. "Wash up. It will soon be ready."

After grace, as they started to eat the simple meal, Fru Nobel looked at her three sons proudly. Fine boys, all of them — so bright, and Robert and Ludwig so healthy. If only Alfred were a little stronger!

Life was not easy in the little gray home set behind the houses which faced the street. For four years now the father had been away, trying his fortune first in Finland, then in the great country of Russia. Things had gone badly for him in Stockholm, and he had said that there was no place in Sweden for an architect and inventor.

Fru Nobel often thought back to the earlier days of

her married life. Immanuel Nobel, a trained engineer with a flair for inventing, had turned architect and had been very successful at it. He had worked on several important houses and buildings and a floating bridge. After marriage the couple had lived in a pleasant apartment in a nice section of the city. Both of the older boys were born there and, as little fellows, they had everything they needed.

Then things changed. There was a fire in one of Immanuel Nobel's buildings. Investments collapsed. Overnight the successful architect became a failure. The proud, ambitious Immanuel Nobel was a bankrupt man without work or money or credit. The family moved to a back-court house and here, that fall of 1833, Alfred was born. A sickly baby, Fru Nobel reflected; they never thought they would pull him through. Yet she remembered with a smile that during all his sicknesses Alfred never whined or fussed. And he was always so affectionate!

Immanuel had set up a small factory for rubber goods — various sorts of small appliances — with Ludwig Ahlsell, his brother-in-law, backing him financially. And he had tried inventing again. He invented a rubber bag which soldiers could carry their equipment in and then blow up to make a sort of rubber boat when they needed to cross a stream. But the Swedish Army did not think much of this novel idea, and once again Immanuel was thwarted, though not for long. Immanuel Nobel was not the kind of person to be held down by misfortune. Sweden, he decided, was just not the place for a man with ideas; his fortune lay in some other country, perhaps Finland.

Much as his wife hated to have him leave, she realized that it was not good for him to stay where he owed money and where he felt there were no opportunities for him. She was sorry when he seemed to have no luck in Finland. In spite of her confidence in him, she worried when he wrote that he had met an influential Russian army man and had gone on with him to St. Petersburg. There, Immanuel wrote, prospects were good and he would soon be sending for her and the children. How she hoped he was right! Four years of separation, with only a few hasty visits, were four years too many.

It was only through her brother Ludwig's constant help that the little household was able to get along.

All day Fru Nobel cooked and cleaned and sewed for her three growing boys. Robert and Ludwig brought in a little money from their part-time jobs, but she would not let them neglect their school to earn more. On that subject she and their father and her brother were agreed — whatever the cost, whatever the sacrifice, the boys should all have a good education. They might not be so well dressed as most of the children in the excellent Jacobs Preparatory School they attended, but their minds, she was certain, were as good as or better than any there.

All three of the Nobel boys liked school, but Alfred fairly ate it up. In December he brought home his first report. Out of the eighty-two pupils in his class he was one of four with a mark of A for "general intelligence." He had an A for industry, too, and also an A for conduct. Fru Nobel was proud but not at all surprised.

"Your father will be pleased," she told her youngest boy, and Alfred's pale cheeks flushed with pleasure.

"It's better than I did!" Ludwig gave his brother a friendly pinch.

Robert patted his shoulder a trifle patronizingly, in

the manner of an older brother. But he was as proud as the others of the new scholar in the family.

Unfortunately, Alfred did not have an A for attendance. He was troubled with many headaches and colds, a poor digestion, and a weak back. There were days and more days when, in spite of a grim determination, he was not able to set out for school. Then he would lie on the couch reading, drawing, and working out in his active mind all sorts of mechanical devices. Sometimes he would talk about them to his brothers and sometimes he would try them out with whatever equipment he could find in the little house. He would read aloud to his mother as she sewed and mended and knitted. A close companionship developed between them — a delightful, affectionate companionship which never faded.

Fru Nobel was a wise woman and a good mother. She had taught each of the boys their letters and something about numbers before they went to school. Now she listened to their ideas and laughed at their jokes. She did not often punish them, especially Alfred. He was smaller than the boys of his age and frailer, and she still sometimes wondered if he would grow to

In comparison, beautiful, orderly Sweden seemed heaven to her. And St. Petersburg, built at the whim of an emperor on low-lying marshes at the head of the Gulf of Finland and the mouth of the Neva River, would be such an unhealthy place to live! Even Immanuel, wrapped up in his work and plans and not one to notice the climate, mentioned the frequent rain and fog and chilly dampness. How would their youngest boy get along there? Alfred was sickly and frail even in healthy Stockholm. Yet at all cost — even in foreign, unhealthy St. Petersburg — the family must be reunited as soon as possible.

During Alfred's first year at school the letters from the father became more and more encouraging. He had been wise, he said, to tie up with the Russian army officer. Russia needed new war equipment if it was to keep its place as Europe's top military power. An idea of his had struck the officer so favorably that he had put it before the czar, Nicholas I, who was considering it. The next letter told of tests.

"What sort of tests?" Ludwig wanted to know. Fru Nobel reread part of her husband's letter, then looked at her sons a little helplessly. Robert and Alfred were waiting for her answer, too. "I don't understand it very well," she admitted. "Something to do with torpedoes, or mines — something that explodes in the sea. On land, too, I believe."

The boys began to discuss the subject of mines and just what the tests might involve. Their mother only half heard them. She was thinking that her sons — all of them — had inherited their father's mechanical, inventive bent. Less and less could she keep up with their technical talk! "What troubles me," she said aloud, "is that this kind of thing sounds dangerous for your father."

"Don't worry, Mother," the boys reassured her. "He'll be all right!" And their eyes shone with admiration of their capable, fearless father.

At last, early in the fall of 1842, came the letter which Fru Nobel and the boys had waited for so long. With it was a sizable amount of money. The czar had advanced the sum Immanuel Nobel had asked for making the tests. As soon as possible, he directed, the little house should be given up and dismantled and tickets bought for St. Petersburg. There a house and a big welcome were waiting for them.

Robert, thirteen now, had other ideas. He had heard of an opening for a cabin boy on a cargo ship sailing to the Mediterranean. He reminded his mother that his father had been only a year older when he had done this very thing. And it would be less expensive, he suggested, for three people to go to Russia than four.

Fru Nobel consulted her brother and wrote her husband. Ludwig Ahlsell investigated the shipping firm, the ship, and the captain, and found them all trustworthy. Somewhat to her disappointment, both her brother and husband agreed that such a voyage would not do Robert a bit of harm and might rid him of his yen for the sea, as it had his father before him.

Alfred did not like being taken out of school just as the fall term was getting well under way. But he was glad they would be with his father and it was exciting to think of living in a foreign country.

In late October, Robert set sail on his voyage to the Mediterranean. A few days later, Fru Nobel, with eleven-year-old Ludwig and nine-year-old Alfred, waved good-by to the Ahlsells from the deck of the St. Petersburg steamer and sailed out of Stockholm harbor into the Baltic Sea.

2

Growing Up
in
Russia

ALFRED AND LUDWIG clung to the rail beside their mother. They looked with wonder at the brown islands and low-lying mainland as the Gulf of Finland narrowed into the Neva River. The damp air was filled with the chill of autumn. Alfred shivered with cold and excitement. Without a word his mother took off her shawl and wrapped it about his shoulders.

The steamship whistled and slowed. It was approaching a stone wharf, loaded with boxes and barrels. A group of men and women stood beside them, waiting for the boat to dock. Sailors threw out heavy ropes from the ship to make it fast, and impatient passengers began to pick up their belongings.

"There he is!" Ludwig's shrill shout rose above the noise.

Alfred strained his eyes. Then they lighted up. "Father!" he called loudly.

The large, vigorous-looking man with the clean-cut features and restless manner caught sight of them and waved.

Fru Nobel and the two boys moved toward the place where the gangplank was being put out. Soon they were on the wharf and wrapped in Immanuel Nobel's welcoming arms. He picked up their bags and led them to the waiting droshky. "I'll send for the trunks and other things later," he said. "Now we'll go to our new home."

They drove some distance down a wide street and past a large open square gay with fall flowers. Nearby a bronze statue of Peter the Great on horseback stood before a half-completed cathedral. In the residential section of St. Petersburg, Herre Nobel proudly unlocked the door of a gray stone house. It was much finer than the house they had left behind in Stockholm. The boys ran from room to room, exclaiming over everything, to their father's delight. Fru Nobel's eyes shone as she saw the comforts of this new home. Perhaps, she decided, life in Russia would not be so bad after all!

The family quickly settled down into a routine pattern of life. For Fru Nobel, it was almost completely domestic; she liked it that way. She hummed as she worked about the house, readjusting small pieces of furniture, dusting the familiar pictures and vases and lamps, and cooking Immanuel's favorite Swedish dishes. There was a maid to help her now, and the two soon managed to understand each other fairly well in spite of each one's knowing only a few words of the other's language.

Immanuel was absorbed in his work, as always. He paid little attention to the life of the city outside his factory and his home. There were many Swedes in St. Petersburg, as well as Finns, Germans, French, and English. The Nobels went to the little Swedish church and made some friends among its members. They were a religious family; the Bible was a familiar and revered book in their home, and the Swedish pastor was their good friend and adviser. With the exception of the church, they had few outside interests. Theirs was a closely knit, companionable, home-centered family life.

The two boys found living in a foreign country immensely exciting. Best of all was having a father again. And such a father! Immanuel Nobel was genuinely interested in them and their ideas. They would talk together by the hour, like three adults, about some mechanical theory or a contraption Ludwig or Alfred had made. However different or "impossible," the father considered it seriously. He was willing to discuss anything they brought up, and whatever he knew he wanted to pass on to them. He was determined that his sons should learn all they could, as soon as they could.

Though the Russian language was not at all like the Swedish, neither of the boys had any trouble with it. Alfred especially seemed to have a talent for the language, and soon he was outstripping Ludwig and even his father in his use of it. Among the Swedish group in St. Petersburg was a well-educated young man who was at home not only in the Swedish language, literature, and history but in the Russian and English also. Immanuel Nobel engaged him as a tutor for the boys. Each day he came to the Nobel house and for several hours tutored the two boys in languages, history, and mathematics.

When, after a few months, Robert joined the family, all three boys studied with the Swedish tutor. Robert did not have too much to say about his voyage. As his father had predicted, he came back rid of his yearning for the sea and content to spend the rest of his life on land.

A year after the family's arrival in St. Petersburg, another boy was born to the household. He was christened Emil Oskar, and he became the pet of them all. Alfred was ten now; Ludwig, twelve; and Robert, fourteen.

All three of the older boys were keenly interested in their father's work and in his factory and foundry. These were situated in the industrial part of the city, across the Neva River from the residential section. Since there was no bridge handy, Herre Nobel was rowed across in a boat each day, except during the long winter months. Then, from November to April, the Neva was frozen so solidly that he could walk over it or drive across in a carriage or sleigh.

The factory was a lively place, and the boys loved to hang around it. Almost every day they managed to get over there. Their father encouraged them to come, after their home studying was done. He showed them around, let them watch experiments, and talked freely to them.

"You understand the problem, don't you?" he asked them. "You know that we are making mines for the Russian Army, but do you realize that we are doing something new, something scientifically important? Not that mines themselves are new; the American Robert Fulton made them thirty years ago. But the old mines were only explosive charges made up on the spot where they were used. We make up the mines ahead of time in the factory, and make them much more accurately than the old ones. Our mines are ready for use when they are needed. They can be placed outside a city, across an important road or railroad track, or in front of a bridge, to protect the city from enemy attack. Or they can be put under water in a harbor that may be entered by enemy ships. Our job is to manufacture large quantities of these mines, and also to try constantly to make them better — more powerful and more certain to explode."

He showed the boys where the gunpowder, made of saltpeter, or niter, charcoal, and sulfur, was mixed. And he explained how these three ingredients, when burned under pressure, provided the gases which interacted to produce the explosion. The difficult thing was to light the gunpowder. This was done in different ways, according to where the mine was to be used. Mines which were buried on land had small caps sticking out at the top. A slight blow would knock one of these caps off, releasing a short chain which was attached to a glass tube of sulfuric acid. This tube would break with the pull and spill onto a mixture of chlorate of potash and sugar, producing enough heat to set off the powder packed below it.

"A big explosion caused by a little one," Herre Nobel told his sons.

Mines anchored in water had long iron poles sticking out of their sides, or were coupled together with chains. When a ship hit the pole or the chain, it smashed the sulfuric-acid tube, with the same result as in the land mines.

The boys could see all sorts of interesting possibilities in the materials and methods used in the factory. They were full of suggestions for changes in the shapes of the mines, in the metals of which they were made, and in the proportions of the chemicals used. They made sketches, which their father went over carefully, complimenting them on their imagination and mechanical ability and explaining why certain things would not work out.

Testing the mines was risky business, but Immanuel Nobel scoffed at the danger. "If you know what you're doing and keep your head, you're all right," he told the boys. They watched with the keenest interest when one day, two years after their arrival in St. Petersburg, he buried a mine and then exploded it before some skeptical army men. It exploded with such power that the men became convinced of its value. On the strength of this test Immanuel Nobel was given a large contract with the Russian Army, to supply them with his mines. The test brought him a partner, too, in the shape of the Russian general who had first been interested in the Swedish inventor's ideas.

The general now became a sort of contact person with the Russian military authorities, and a very successful one. He interested not only the key people in the Army in the Nobel mines but even the czar himself. Nicholas I decided that land and sea mines would be ideal weapons for Russia's defense, and he approved the Army's financing the "alien Nobel" and giving him free rein to develop his ideas.

Never before had the Nobels been so well off. There was money enough for everything they wanted in the way of living comforts and even luxuries. The house was handsomely furnished; Fru Nobel had servants; fruits and special foods were imported for the table. Best of all, every cent of Immanuel Nobel's long-standing bankruptcy debt in Sweden was paid back.

In addition to his military inventions, Immanuel Nobel invented and produced some things for civilian use. One of them added considerably to the family comfort during the intensely cold winters. It was a hot-water heating system which Herre Nobel installed first in his own house, then in several hotels, hospitals, and elegant private homes.

The damp, changeable climate of St. Petersburg certainly was no help to Alfred's health. Here, as in

Stockholm, he was sick much of the time. He hated the days when the pain in his back or a headache or an upset stomach forced him to stay home, while Robert and Ludwig went off to the factory. But even stretched out on a bed or couch, he made good use of his time. Since languages were easy for him, he was soon able to read and speak in French and English besides, of course, Swedish and Russian. After the Swedish tutor had given place to a Russian one, Alfred added German to his language repertory and, later, Italian. He read many Swedish and English novels and also much English poetry. The poems of Byron and Shelley he liked especially well. But science was his greatest interest. In this field he read everything he could lay his hands on. With this wide background, added to the practical knowledge gained in his father's plant, Alfred Nobel was a competent industrial chemist by the time he was sixteen.

Alfred had grown more slowly than his older brothers, but at fifteen he had taken a sudden spurt and within a year stretched up to almost medium height. He suddenly had more physical energy, too. Once, when he couldn't find a boat to take him across the river to the factory, he stripped off most of his clothes and swam over. When his brothers poked fun at him rather harshly about this impulsive action, he grew angry. Ridicule was the one thing he could not stand, and he decided that his brothers must learn not to make fun of him. Confiding only in his mother, he packed a knapsack and took off eastward, toward the great Russian interior. He was gone for two weeks.

All his life Alfred Nobel liked, when he could, to get away from people and to be alone among trees and plants. "Silent friends who do not get on my nerves," he called them. He was fond of Byron's lines, which he knew by heart:

> There is a pleasure in the pathless woods,
> There is a rapture on the lonely shore,
> There is society, where none intrudes,
> By the deep sea, and music in its roar;
> I love not man the less, but nature more . . .

While things were going so well for the Nobel family, most of the people in Russia were not faring at all well. The peasants, or little farmers, who made up most of the population outside of the big cities, were having such a hard time that they rose up in revolt. Nicholas

I ruled with an iron hand; he crushed these peasant uprisings with great cruelty. He imposed censorship, discouraged progress, and winked at graft in high places in order to get money to develop a well-equipped, well-trained army and navy. It was for this reason that he encouraged the activities of the "alien Nobel." Immanuel Nobel knew very well that the czar would not hesitate to turn to any other inventor who could surpass him. This thought, as well as his own natural instinct, kept him constantly trying to improve his product.

When Alfred was sixteen, Ludwig eighteen, and Robert twenty, their father decided the time had come for them to end their school days and really get down to business. He dismissed the Russian tutor and took Robert and Ludwig into the firm. Ludwig, who had great mechanical ability, was to work in the factory; Robert, who had a flair for business expansion and development, was to work on outside contacts. Each of them received a good salary. The father proudly wrote of Robert, "Thank God, I can say he earns it." He could surely have said the same of Ludwig, for this second son was both capable and industrious.

So was Alfred. But since he was the youngest, had a talent for languages, and still was not strong, he was sent on an extensive rich-man's-son tour. It was not completely without its connection with the business. Alfred was instructed to make acquaintances and contacts which might be helpful to them, and to keep his eyes open for scientific developments which would improve their products or add to them.

And so for two years Alfred traveled. He went first to Germany, then to Denmark, and from there, by boat, to Italy. He stayed at fashionable hotels, met many people, saw many things. But he soon wearied of luxurious living, of casual acquaintances, and of tourist sights. He especially disliked the artificial, semisocial atmosphere of the spas, the health resorts, which he visited in the vain hope of improving his uncertain health. Yet he continued to go to them, every few months, all his life.

When he traveled north to Paris, he did not spend his time, as many young men might have done, in the cafés or theaters or art galleries. Instead, he sought out the laboratories. Interesting experiments were going on in Paris at that time, and Alfred Nobel had a talent for uncovering them and following up the significant ones. Théophile Pelouze, who had discovered some new things in the explosives field, including guncotton, was a professor at the Polytechnical School and the College of France and also conducted a laboratory school on the side. Alfred would far rather put in his time there than on the fashionable boulevards or in "arty" Montmartre.

But there were many days when he felt wretched and many evenings when he was lonely. At these times, Alfred covered page after page with his poetical efforts. He was not entirely sure that he wanted to be a chemist or industrial engineer. He thought he might prefer to be a poet. Strangely, he wrote in English rather than in Swedish or Russian. This was due in part to the tremendous impression made on him by the English poets, Byron and Shelley. Though both of them were long dead, their poems were still widely read not only in England but all over Europe and America. Alfred, introspective and often depressed himself, felt sympathetic toward Byron's sensitive, cynical soul and was drawn even more to Shelley. By nature he too was an idealist, a believer in a good God and in a mankind ever struggling toward peace and happiness. Like Shelley, he "could scorn hate, and pride, and fear."

To make himself more proficient in the English language Alfred would translate both poetry and prose into Swedish and then retranslate it into English and compare it with the original. He did this with French literature too, often using Victor Hugo as his model. In this way he came to know both these languages as intimately as anyone not born in England or France could know them.

Alfred Nobel's poems were long, involved, philosophical, and not very good. He threw most of them away. One, a lengthy autobiographical work, he saved. It had, for a young man, an unnatural concern with death, yet perhaps not so unnatural considering his poor health and the somewhat morbid nature of the Russian people he had lived among. It told of his disillusionment with his travels and, most interesting, of his falling in love with a beautiful girl who loved him in return. He wrote of feeling:

> Supremely happy, and we met again,
> And oft again till we had grown to be
> A heaven to one another.

And then, alas, the girl died.

> And from that hour
> I have not shared the pleasures of the crowd
> Nor moved in Beauty's eye compassion's tear,
> But I have learned to study Nature's book
> And comprehend its pages, and extract
> From their deep lore solace for my grief.

No one ever knew who the girl was — or even whether, perhaps, the romance was all in Alfred Nobel's imaginative mind, a poetic dream.

From Paris, after many months, Alfred went to London. There he attended the theater and the first great International Exhibition held in Crystal Palace. And from England he sailed across the Atlantic to America. Here for several months he stayed in New York City, at the place where John Ericsson lived — the same John Ericsson who later invented the *Monitor* of Civil War fame, and who then was working on steamship projects. He and Alfred's father had studied under the same engineering professor in Stockholm, years before — and Immanuel Nobel was not one to let such a contact go untapped.

His mind and notebooks full of information, Alfred was ready now to return to St. Petersburg. The journey east seemed never-ending, so eager was he to be home again. His two years away had been full to the brim; they had changed him from a boy into a man. He knew now beyond doubt what he wanted to be. Not a poet, but a scientist. He would concentrate all his energies to that end. With this in mind, he reread the lines he had written in Paris about life:

> I look upon it as a noble gift,
> A gem from Nature's hand for man to polish
> Till sparkling beams repay him for his toil.

3

Atéliers
Méchaniques,
Nobel & Fils

ALFRED'S FIRST EVENING at home was a happy time.
His father and brothers greeted him warmly and his
mother hugged him tight, wiping from her eyes tears
of joy and relief. He exclaimed at the way young Emil
had grown; there was a big difference between the six-
year-old boy he had left and the eight-year-old one he
found on his return. At first Emil was a little shy with
this half-forgotten brother, but soon he followed him
about from room to room and hung over him as he unpacked his bulging bags. There were gifts in them for
everyone from the strange big city of New York, far
across the ocean.

At supper Fru Nobel served the foods Alfred liked

best. Afterward Emil was allowed to stay up way past his bedtime as they all gathered around to listen to Alfred's experiences in different countries. Herre Nobel was especially interested to hear of his old schoolmate John Ericsson, who, like himself, had left his native Sweden to try his fortune in another land. Ericsson had gone west, while he had come east, Immanuel mused. He was fascinated by Alfred's reports of the iron ships Ericsson was designing, and the screw propellers to replace the old steamship side wheels, and even vessels which would travel beneath the surface of the water.

After the gifts had been distributed and young Emil had gone unwillingly to bed, Alfred began to ask questions. How were things going at the factory? Were they busy? Were they trying anything new?

The father winked at the two oldest sons. "Wait till morning," he said, and when Alfred turned to Robert and Ludwig, they said the same thing. Alfred wondered at all the pleasant secrecy, but he was too weary to pry into it.

The next morning, when the four of them arrived together at the plant, Alfred discovered some of the answers. He whistled his astonishment at the size of the factory; it had been enlarged to almost twice the size he had known. Then, as the others watched him, laughing, he looked in unbelief at the sign over the door: ATÉLIERS MÉCHANIQUES, NOBEL & FILS. The fancy French "Mechanical Studios" did not stop him half so much as the "Nobel and Sons."

"What does it mean?" he asked. "Where is the general?"

The general, Alfred's father told him, had left to take over some special military assignment for the czar. "And so" — and Herre Nobel said this with considerable pride — "this all belongs to us, to the Nobel family. And you, Alfred, are a full-fledged member of the firm."

Alfred was speechless, but his eyes showed his pleasure.

All that morning either his father or Robert or Ludwig had him in tow, showing him this change and that, explaining new methods, telling of huge government orders.

"Why this rush of business?" Alfred wanted to know.

"Because of the national situation," his father told him. "Nicholas I has great ideas of expansion," he said in a low voice, speaking in Swedish and careful to stand at a distance from the workmen. "He keeps stretching the country farther and farther southward. You know how, a few years ago, through threats and wars and treaties, he won the Black Sea for Russia. Since then he has been gaining more and more control over Turkey. He means to win through to the Mediterranean," Herre Nobel whispered, "and for that, Russia must be strong. That is why we have such large government orders for mines."

"Is that all the factory is producing?" Alfred asked. "Mines?"

"No, we do some other things. Ludwig will show you. But civilians are not such good customers as the czar," Herre Nobel chuckled.

Ludwig took Alfred to the part of the foundry where Russian workmen were making wheels, iron pipes, machine parts, and the hot-water heaters Immanuel Nobel had invented. It was not so large or so busy a place, Alfred noticed, as the part devoted to the manufacture of mines.

Alfred threw himself head over heels into the work of the factory. All day, every day, regardless of how he felt, he went to the Atéliers Méchaniques with his father and brothers. There he tried out chemicals, supervised tests, and worked on mechanical improvements for the principal product — mines — and for the side lines intended for peacetime uses. At night he pored over the pages of notes he had made in Paris and in New York. There were so many things he wanted to do, and the family factory was an ideal place to do them. His father and two older brothers were ready to listen to his ideas. They were all agreed that Nobel & Fils should make nothing less than the best, and that perfecting their products was a big and important part of their job.

For Alfred it was a fascinating scientific challenge. He turned on it all the power of his inventive mind, his ability for concentration, and his capacity for hard work. He thought of the mines as a theoretical problem and did not dwell on the deadly uses they would be put to. They were a defensive weapon, Immanuel Nobel often explained. This made them a constructive contribution to civilization, and the more destructive they were, the better they could protect cities against enemy attack and invasion.

One great improvement was the use of guncotton in place of gunpowder. Alfred had encountered this new explosive in Paris, where Professor Pelouze had taken the first steps in developing it. The professor had noticed that cotton soaked in strong, cold nitric acid became much heavier, and that after it had dried, it had explosive properties. Guncotton, being a chemical compound, was better than gunpowder, because each molecule contained within itself the elements that would combine to form the gas which produced the explosion. The old gunpowder, or "black powder," as it was called, was only a mechanical mixture. Each single particle of the saltpeter had to attack some single particle of the combustible sulfur and carbon to cause the explosion, which could fail if the proportions were not just right or if the ingredients were not thoroughly mixed. To be sure, the cotton had to be carefully cleaned to free the cellulose fiber from rubbish and carefully dried to rid it of its natural dampness, which would dilute the acids. But the resulting explosion was both more dependable and more powerful than the gunpowder explosion. Another advantage, the guncotton would ignite at a lower temperature.

Alfred became engrossed with the possibilities of this new explosive. He spent days and weeks in the factory laboratory working with it. One day two chemistry professors from the University of St. Petersburg brought in another explosive substance and showed it to Immanuel Nobel. One of them, Professor Zinin, was regarded very highly, Alfred knew, both as a teacher and as an able scientist. Alfred paid close attention. The explosive was in liquid form. The professors called it nitroglycerin and said it had been discovered a few years earlier by an Italian chemist who had not continued to work with it because its high explosive properties made it too dangerous. Immanuel Nobel was interested. He promised to make some tests with the nitroglycerin. And he did, but as they were not particularly successful, he did not go on with it.

Together father and sons talked over the problems of Nobel & Fils and worked both jointly and individually to solve them. They were a hard-working family. None of them closed his eyes or mind to new opportunities or scientific possibilities. Ludwig, the father thought, had the most genius; Robert, the greatest courage in speculation; Alfred, the most industry. It was probably Robert who advised his father to take a more active interest in the affairs of the city and encouraged him to join the first Merchants Guild of St. Petersburg.

There was great excitement in the Nobel household when Herre and Fru Nobel received a formal invitation to a great reception at the court of Nicholas I, Czar of Russia. There, among all the high-born ladies dressed in the height of French fashion and the grand gentlemen brilliant with ribbons and medals, Herre Nobel and his wife were presented to the czar. Herre Nobel was proud of his sweet-faced wife, her grayish-blond hair worn simply in a coronet braid, her gown the handsomest she had ever had. To their surprise, Nicholas I put about the neck of the Swedish engineer the Imperial Gold Medal in token of his services to the Crown. In addition, as a more personal gift, the czar gave the "alien Nobel" a valuable watch.

The Nobels could hardly wait to get home to show their trophies to the family. Much as he appreciated the favor of the czar, Immanuel Nobel preferred the affectionate admiration of his four sons.

In spite of the factory sign, in spite of the time and talent his three oldest sons contributed to the success of the firm, the father still made most of the decisions. Now, fully assured of royal support, he went ahead with a wider expansion of the plant. He put back into the business practically all the profits he had made in the last few prosperous years. He borrowed money and built; he borrowed more money and bought equipment and materials; he borrowed still more money and hired more workers, until over a thousand employees were on the payroll. There was no end in sight to the prosperity of Nobel & Fils.

Only Fru Nobel worried about the future. "Suppose the Army should cancel its orders? Suppose the czar should die? Suppose something should go wrong?"

Her husband reassured her. "How can it?" he asked. "The whole Russian Government is behind us, and my contracts are in writing, not just in my head."

Nicholas I, whether he realized it or not, was rushing head-on into war. The western European nations had not objected when Russia had pretty much imposed its will on Moslem Turkey, because Russia, like them, was a Christian nation, though of the Eastern Orthodox faith. But Nicholas put too much trust in their silence. He did not realize that Great Britain and France were becoming alarmed at Russia's growing power.

The czar was astonished when the English and French suddenly changed sides after he destroyed the Turkish fleet on some slight pretext. He was amazed at their open admiration of the Turks' resistance. And dumfounded when, in 1854, Great Britain and France decided to come to the relief of Turkey. They declared war on Russia, and other European nations joined them. The allied troops sailed across the Mediterranean and up into the Black Sea. There they landed on the peninsula which juts south from Russia into that sea — the Crimea.

Then came the struggle known as the Crimean War. It was in this war that Florence Nightingale's name became world famous because of all she did for the wounded English soldiers hospitalized far away from home. The Russians had no one like her; thousands of their men died on their march south through the trackless deserts and forests of southern Russia. It was much harder for Russia to get its soldiers and supplies to the Crimean battleground by land than for the allies to bring theirs in by sea.

The allies sent a fleet of British and French ships into the Gulf of Finland, intending to bring the Russians to their knees by invading their northern cities. They would capture first Kronstadt, Sveaborg, and Reval, the British thought, and then go on to St. Petersburg. But Immanuel Nobel's mines, installed by Robert Nobel, helped put a stop to that idea. The allied fleet commander, seeing the Kronstadt harbor filled with strange devices, detailed his next in command and a seaman to pull one of them out. When it exploded, killing the seaman and wounding the second-in-command, the crew was filled with fear of the deadly machines. The allied ship commanders, too, developed such a healthy respect for the sea mines and the city fortifications that they made no further attempt to enter the harbor. And so the Nobel mines not only helped protect northern Russian cities from attack, but they released Russian soldiers from their defense, making them available to join their comrades at Sevastopol, in the Crimea.

The allies had a great advantage over the Russians in their steamships. Russia had only old-time sailing vessels. She needed the more modern equipment badly. The government offered Nobel & Fils a contract to build steam engines to put into the old sailing ships. The fact that he did not know the first thing about building steam engines did not stop Immanuel Nobel. He signed the contract, knowing that he could not import a thing — neither materials, nor tools, nor experienced workmen. He would have to design his own tools and train Russian workers, not one of whom had ever worked on a steam engine. In fact, few of them had ever even seen one!

Alfred searched his notebooks and his memory for every helpful detail from his visit with John Ericsson. All the Nobels worked day and night. Within a year the firm made and turned over to the Russian Government eight steam engines — and then they made three more. It was an incredible achievement.

Besides the steam engines, Nobel & Fils took on contracts for making cannon and other war equipment.

Some was manufactured in the Atéliers Méchaniques, but more was made in other factories on subcontracts given out by the Nobels and by men trained by them.

Alfred worked so hard that his uncertain health gave way. In the summer of 1854, his family insisted that he take a vacation. He went first to his relatives in Sweden. On the shores of Lake Mälar, near Stockholm, he loafed with his cousins' families. He had long talks with his Uncle Ludwig, to whom he was devoted, and he chatted with his old grandmother. From Stockholm he went on to a famous health resort in Bohemia, where he took the baths, drank the water, and walked and rested. But he wrote the Ahlsells that his visit with them did him more good than all the waters and cures at the Bohemian spa. On his way home he stopped in Berlin on business for the firm. He did not linger, for he wanted to get back in time to be with his family for his twenty-first birthday, on October 21, 1854.

Right away he plunged into work again. But what he thought of the Crimean War or of making weapons for it, he did not say. Though he wrote often to his uncle and cousins in Sweden, he never mentioned the war or the "inner chasm" that was developing in him between his love of his work, which was concerned with deadly weapons, and his natural love of peace. The family — and Nobel & Fils — were glad to have him back. In a letter to his brother-in-law and friend, Ludwig Ahlsell, Immanuel Nobel said that they all depended on Alfred for "his knowledge and his tireless energy."

After holding out for a year on the Crimean peninsula, with tremendous courage and loyalty, the Russian soldiers there finally lost the stronghold of Sevastopol to the allied armies of western Europe. Nicholas I did not live to see this humiliation. He died a few months before it happened, and his oldest son became Czar Alexander II. Alexander had no wish to prolong the war which was going so badly for the Russians. He could see the need to modernize Russia to bring it up to the level of the Western powers. He wanted to make many social reforms within the country, and in order to get at this work without delay, he agreed to a peace treaty with the allies. This treaty, signed in Paris in 1856, limited Russia's territories and her activities on the Black Sea. Russia had not been completely defeated, but her pride had been broken and her power curtailed enough to satisfy the allies.

The new czar planned to avoid all entanglements with other nations while he built up his country. And so he gave no more orders to Nobel & Fils. Not only that, but he canceled those which the government had already contracted for. Immanuel Nobel put in claims for compensation. They were completely disregarded. Nothing he could do or say had the slightest weight with the authorities; the czar's word was law.

Fru Nobel's fears began to come true. Nobel & Fils had borrowed heavily on the strength of the government contracts. Now creditors started to press for their money. A fire in the plant made bad matters worse.

During this difficult time, in 1857, Alfred Nobel applied for and received his first patent. It was for a gas meter based on determining the quantity of water or alcohol which the gas would absorb. It was not a very practical device, and nothing came of it.

The Nobels were at their wits' end. They curtailed production and dismissed workmen right and left. They tried to get credit through influential circles in

Russia, but could not. Neither could they get any financial help in Sweden. Nobel's old bankruptcy record, though long since settled in full, was against him. Besides, wealthy Swedes just were not interested in investing in a machinery plant in Russia, even if it were changed over entirely to civilian products.

The family decided that Alfred, with his contacts in other countries and his fluency in other languages, should go to England and, if necessary, to France to try to raise money for the firm. And so, four years after his journey to Sweden and Bohemia for a healthful rest, Alfred started out again. This was no vacation trip. The fate of Nobel & Fils was in his hands.

He went first to London. But he could find no one there interested in helping finance a factory in Russia. Neither for producing the deadly devices which had stopped British ships in the recent war nor for manufacturing products for civilian use.

He went on to Paris. Things seemed a little more hopeful there. Napoleon III was by nature a speculator, and the whole country was bursting with money-making schemes which the influx of gold from California and Australia had made possible. For a time

Alfred thought he would get in France the financial help Nobel & Fils so badly needed. Then hope flew out the window. At last Alfred had to admit failure. He returned to St. Petersburg either completely empty-handed or at best with too little, too late.

Early in 1859, Immanuel Nobel locked the doors of the family factory for the last time and, with a heavy heart, turned the keys over to his creditors. To make things darker, Alfred became seriously ill, worn out with the strain of his work, travels, and unsuccessful money-raising efforts. For weeks his life was in danger. His parents gave him every attention, in spite of their other cares and anxieties. They sold the big house and its fine furnishings and used every penny to satisfy their creditors and pay the expenses of Alfred's illness. Herre Nobel even pawned the gold watch the old czar had given him.

As soon as they were sure that Alfred would re-cover, Herre and Fru Nobel and fifteen-year-old Emil left for Sweden. The three oldest sons stayed on in St. Petersburg. Ludwig had been employed by the Nobel & Fils creditors to run the business until it was sold. He was an excellent mechanical engineer, a steady, industrious young man of twenty-eight. The previous year he had married a Swedish cousin and soon after the family separation there was a baby, Emanuel. The little family lived in a small flat, while Robert and Alfred shared a room in a big house nearby. They all lived very cheaply, in great contrast to their life a few years before.

Robert found work on a building job, and when he discovered some interesting clay near the city, he started a small ceramics plant on the side. He also acquired an old sailboat, installed a steam engine in it, and rented it out for pleasure trips on the Gulf of Finland. This was not as profitable as he had hoped, and he considered turning the pleasure boat into a floating sawmill!

For months Alfred, much to his disgust, was not able to do anything to bring in money. He tried his hand at writing novels and turned out two — *Brothers and Sisters* and *In Brightest Africa*. But his language (he wrote in Swedish) was stilted and he could not make his characters come alive. He was more interested in setting forth his religious and political ideas than in telling a story. As soon as he was able,

Alfred went into the little machine shop which Ludwig had managed to buy with money saved from his salary and which he ran on the side.

Soon after their parents and Emil had left, Robert fell in love with a Finnish girl. Pauline did not like living in Russia. Robert promised her that if she would marry him, he would take her back to Finland to live. And so that next year he and Alfred gave up their room. Robert married and went with his bride to Finland. Alfred joined Ludwig and his young wife and baby.

Cheerful letters came from the father in Stockholm. The family had rented a small house in the Heleneborg section of Stockholm and he was using a room in it as a laboratory-workroom. He was experimenting with many new inventions, most of them connected with mines. One idea was to make his sea mines movable by using trained seals to drag them to the desired locations. This plan he confided in a letter to Robert, in Finland. Perhaps he felt that Robert, being of a more speculative turn of mind, would be more sympathetic to it than either Ludwig or Alfred. The father asked Robert's help in getting the seals. Robert sent the letter to his brothers in St. Petersburg, who advised him to discourage their father from going on with this wild idea.

Then there came a letter from Stockholm to Alfred. This sounded much more practical. It told of work on new explosives, with a view to making the mines far more powerful. Herre Nobel reminded Alfred of Professor Zinin and the other St. Petersburg professor who had brought them an "explosive oil" called nitroglycerin some years before. The tests on it then had not been successful, but now, in trying out the combination of various acids with gunpowder, he had retested this oil and found it very effective. In fact, Immanuel Nobel wrote, it was twenty times as powerful as gunpowder. He asked Alfred to try to interest the Russian Army chiefs in the new product. If they showed any inclination to take it up, Alfred should come to Stockholm for some final tests and then take samples back to the Russian Army authorities.

Alfred went to the inspector general of army engineers, who knew the Nobels and thought highly of Herre Nobel's engineering and inventive skill. He told

Alfred that he would be glad to try out the new powder. The claims Alfred made for it were much more modest that his father's — Alfred knew only too well how his father's enthusiastic nature prodded him into exaggerating a little! Optimistically, Alfred said good-by to Ludwig and crossed the sea to Stockholm. Both of them hoped that something important might come out of this new development.

It was good to be with his father and mother and young Emil again. And it was good to work with his father in the makeshift laboratory in the small house. But the tests were disappointing. Neither the combination of nitroglycerin with gunpowder nor any of the other combinations was anything like the great improvement over the old "black powder" that Immanuel Nobel had claimed for them.

To please his father, Alfred took samples back to St. Petersburg. But when he talked the matter over with Ludwig, they both agreed that for the sake of the family reputation they should not submit the samples to the army men. Yet, since the matter had been opened with them, and the army men were expecting something, both Ludwig and Alfred felt they must make some attempt to pull their father's chestnuts out of the fire.

So Alfred went to work in Ludwig's little machine shop to try to develop a more effective explosive than his father had managed to do. All that spring of 1862, he experimented with one thing and another. He used the same substances — nitroglycerin and gunpowder — but he worked out a new method of exploding them.

By summer Alfred was ready to test his invention. Robert came over from Finland to see the demonstration. Both he and Ludwig had great confidence in Alfred's ability. Now they stood near the machine shop, watching their younger brother set up the test. They saw him put a tightly corked glass tube full of nitroglycerin into a tin can containing gunpowder. They watched him attach a fuse to the powder, cover the can, and stick it deep into a little water-filled ditch. Then they saw him light the fuse and step back. In a few seconds there was an explosion. The ground about the ditch quivered and a stream of liquid shot into the air.

"You see!" Alfred exclaimed, his eyes shining. "It's

not just the gunpowder that exploded. The nitro-glycerin exploded too!"

The brothers were delighted. Alfred should make a few more tests, they said, just to be certain, and provide containers that were not quite so crude — a little polishing up and a little more practice, then he would be ready to put on his demonstration for the army engineers.

And so he did. The army men were pleased, and promised to consider using the new product. But there were the usual delays. Months went by and still a definite offer did not come through from the Army. At any moment, Alfred felt, his invention would be accepted and the turn made in the Nobel fortunes. Meantime he went on with his work for Ludwig and with his experiments.

Then another letter came from the father in Stockholm. He claimed now to have developed a much more effective powder. It was something they could not afford to neglect; it would make them all their fortunes. Alfred must come to Stockholm at once and work with him on it.

Once again Alfred talked the matter over with

Ludwig, and once again they agreed that they could not disappoint their father. Life had handed him too many disappointments already. One of the older sons should go to him and stay with him. Robert was better off in Finland. Ludwig was becoming well established in Russia.

Alfred was obviously the one to go. Besides, he was the one the father had asked for. And so, in the summer of 1863, Alfred left Russia for good and headed for his native Sweden.

4

Alfred
Takes Over

HELENEBORG was a neighborhood of small homes on the edge of Stockholm. The houses were not built too close together; there were still vacant lots and even some old farmsteads, for the city had not yet grown out quite that far. The few neighbors, while not unfriendly, were not particularly warm toward the elderly couple and their teen-age son who came to live in Heleneborg. Rumor had it that this Nobel family had lived like princes in Russia and then had lost everything, which was why they had come back to Stockholm. The hard-working Swedes of Heleneborg did not understand a man who spent long hours fussing around at home every day instead of going out to work. Some of them had seen the room he had fitted up with all sorts of strange glass tubes and jars and equipment, and it seemed like a queer sort of business for an able-bodied man. They were pleasant enough to the Nobels when they met at church on Sunday, but among themselves the neighbors agreed that this was not a home where they would feel free to drop in for morning coffee.

Nor did the Nobels have many old friends in Stockholm; the parents had been away too long, and Emil had never lived in Sweden. There were, of course, Fru Nobel's relatives, but they lived in a different part of the city. Herre Nobel's early home had been in Gävle, a hundred and fifty miles up the coast from Stockholm. He had almost lost touch with his kinsfolk there, for his wife's family had become like his own; her brother Ludwig was as close to him as a blood brother.

Alfred wondered how his parents could be so content in this place which was so different from the elegant house in the fashionable part of St. Petersburg. Yet he knew the answer — his father was so wrapped up in his work and dreams that, given the

minimum comforts, he was almost unconscious of
where he lived. And his mother, Alfred knew, lived
to make life happy for her husband and sons. However
small and inconvenient the house, she would make a
home of it. And so long as she could work at home-
making for her family, she would be content.

Emil was away at college. He had been glad to go.
It had been hard to manage financially, but all the
Nobels — as well as Uncle Ludwig, who was best
able to help — were determined that this youngest
boy should have the advantages of the college education which none of them had had. Not since their
great-great-grandfather, Petrus Nobelius, had a Nobel
graduated from a university. Now all their unfulfilled
academic ambitions were rolled up in this bright, lika-
ble youngest son. Emil, like his father and his brothers,
was interested in science, and particularly in chemistry. He was doing well at the great Swedish university
of Uppsala, as they had known he would do. His
mother missed him at home, but Uppsala was near
enough so Emil could come to Heleneborg for all the
holidays and of course for the long summer vacation.

Fru Nobel gave Alfred Emil's small room and turned

her loving attention to this next older son of hers. She cooked nourishing foods to put meat on his bones and scolded him gently for working such long hours in the makeshift laboratory. That place was a hardship to her; they needed every one of the rooms in the small house for living. But she knew that this was the way it must be until Immanuel got ahead enough to rent a workshop outside. So she reconciled herself to the unpleasant odors, to the running to and from the kitchen sink, and to the chemical stains on her well-scoured floors. The idea that these experiments might be in any way dangerous apparently never occurred to her, or to the others.

Much to Alfred's disappointment, though not entirely to his surprise, his father's new explosive was not the success they all had wanted. Soon after his arrival, Emil came home from college, and that summer of 1863 the three of them — Immanuel, Alfred, and Emil — worked together. They practically turned the whole house into a laboratory as they tested various combinations of gunpowder and nitroglycerin. The powder seemed to lose its strength a few hours after it was mixed. It was Emil who discovered that very fine gunpowder, thoroughly saturated with nitroglycerin and then confined tightly in a small space, gave the best results. Luckily there was plenty of open space nearby where they could set off their rather feeble explosions. Or they could walk to the edge of the lake and listen to the reverberations of the little blasts over the water toward the island where the grim city prison stood. Using lead pipe and other primitive equipment, they tried again and again to bring off a truly powerful explosion. But they never really succeeded.

With his usual impulsive optimism, Immanuel Nobel had gone to the Swedish military authorities and "sold" them on his new explosive powder. They had given him a small sum of money to perfect it and had set the time for a demonstration at an army fortress, before a military commission. Emil had gone back to college before that time came, but Alfred went with his father to the army post. In the heavy guns the finely mixed powder and nitroglycerin did quite well, but when Herre Nobel tried to explode a shell with it, nothing happened. Three times he tried, without success. Then Alfred could stand it no longer. With his father's permission, he changed the proportion of gunpowder and nitroglycerin and packed it more tightly, following Emil's suggestion. This time the shell exploded. Alfred stepped into the background and let his father do the talking with the military experts. They were not encouraging. The new explosive, they said, evidently was not suitable for use in cannon or shells. The Army would not be interested in exploring the matter any further.

Immanuel Nobel was crushed — momentarily. But not Alfred. This gave him the excuse he needed for going back to the approach he had been working on by himself in St. Petersburg. This was the principle of using a first, easily produced explosion to cause a second — the main — explosion. He performed more than fifty experiments, trying to find the best way to bring about the initial explosion which in turn would produce the explosion that would do the work. His father laughed at him for his persistence, but he worked on.

One day, without a word, Alfred took his samples to a granite quarry near Stockholm. He asked the manager's permission to demonstrate a new explosive. Opening the metal case he was carrying, he took from it his simple apparatus with the charge of gunpowder and nitroglycerin ready for use. He buried it deep in a crevice of rock, then lighted the fuse and stepped back to safety with the manager and his men. In a moment or two there was an explosion — a good-sized explosion. When the manager went with Alfred to the spot and saw the size of the rocks dislodged by it, he was immediately interested in this young man's product. It was more effective, he frankly admitted, than anything he had ever used, and it seemed well suited to his blasting needs. Would Mr. Nobel make a few more tests, to make sure this was a not a fluke and that the explosive would work equally well each time?

Mr. Nobel was delighted. He promised to come again within a few days and make another test. On his way home he thought about the whole new field this one experience had opened up. His father had been so accustomed to working with and for military men that he had scoffed at the possibilities of civilian uses for his explosives. But Alfred could see that there was a real need for powerful explosives in quarries, mines, and construction projects. And a big market, too. Filling that need and opening up that market, he knew, would please him much more than producing explosives for military purposes. His father might not think much of it, but it suited him right down to the ground!

That fall Alfred worked ceaselessly on improving his new explosive. Not so much the ingredients, of which nitroglycerin was the essential one, as the method by which the main charge was to be exploded. That was the difficult thing. For this tremendously powerful new explosive could not be fired with a match or fuse, the way gunpowder or guncotton could be. Just adding the nitroglycerin, or pyroglycerin as some called it, to gunpowder might satisfy Immanuel Nobel, but not Alfred. He was determined to find a way to use the full power of the explosive oil. Emil's contribution of sealing the charge in tightly was helpful, but it was not enough.

And so Alfred Nobel decided to improve his method of exploding the nitroglycerin by means of the heat and shock caused by a small explosion next to it. At first he put gunpowder into a glass tube above or below the nitroglycerin. Then he used a tin container loaded with a mixture of gunpowder or nitrate of potash with fulminate of mercury. Still later he used a small copper percussion cap filled with fulminate of mercury alone. This white crystalline substance, formed by the action of a mercurous nitrate solution on alcohol, was more sensitive to friction and more reliable than the other substances or mixtures. But the principle with all of them was the same — a little explosion, caused by a spark or violent blow, setting off a big one. It was the same principle his father had used in his mines, before the days of nitroglycerin.

In October, 1863, Alfred Nobel applied for and was granted a ten-year patent to manufacture his new explosive "in the manner described." This was rather vague, due to the fact that he had written his application without any legal help and also perhaps because he was still thinking his way through the details of his invention. In his application he had given a rather long and involved description of the whole explosive process, mentioning the mixture of nitroglycerin and gunpowder.

In addition to the Swedish patent, Alfred also applied for and was granted patents in Belgium, England, and France. He considered protecting his new explosive in the United States, but when he found that he must state that he was its sole inventor, he gave up the idea, for he considered that his father and his brother Emil had shared in the invention.

Alfred went back to the quarry, as he had promised, and made more satisfactory tests. Then he contacted others — quarry owners, mining engineers, and contractors on large construction projects. His laboratory time became more and more interrupted with demonstrations, sometimes at quite a distance from home. In December he put on a series of tests at the big Ammeberg zinc mines, a bit over a hundred miles southwest of Stockholm. These tests created so much interest that they were reported in the leading Stockholm newspaper and written up in mining journals. The general manager of the Ammeberg mine agreed to try out the new explosive. Alfred suggested that he use it exclusively for two weeks and compare his output with that of the previous two weeks, and then pay for the explosive whatever seemed fair to him.

Herre Nobel could not help noticing all this interest and publicity. At last he grudgingly admitted that a real business could grow out of the explosive's use in mines, quarries, tunnel digging, and on construction jobs where obstacles must be cleared away for new highways or railroads. He agreed to join forces with Alfred and help produce the explosive oil for sale.

Early in 1864, Immanuel Nobel rented a small empty building in the neighborhood. To Fru Nobel's delight, all the chemical equipment was transferred from the house to this new workshop-laboratory-office. With less pleasure, she watched her husband and son disappear in the direction of the building and surmised — correctly — that from now on it would be a second home to them. Except when he was away giving demonstrations or trying to interest some engineer in his invention, Alfred practically lived there. Soon there was so much demand for "Nobel's blasting oil" that a young man was employed to help prepare it. But Alfred was the principal figure in the little group. Though the nitroglycerin gave him violent headaches, though his back ached and his stomach rebelled, he persisted in his chemical research.

All that spring articles continued to appear in newspapers and technical magazines about the remarkable new explosive oil invented by the young Swedish chemist and civil engineer Alfred Nobel. Some of these articles were in periodicals published in other countries — Germany, Belgium, France, and England. As a result, letters began to come into the Nobel office from many places. They asked for more details and wanted to know when this new nitroglycerin explosive would be available for shipment abroad.

Robert, trying to make a living selling lamps and oil in Finland, did not know about all this stir. He wrote a stern letter to Alfred, urging him to give up the foolish business of inventing. "It brings only disappointment," he wrote. "You have such wide knowledge and such unusual talents that you should turn your mind to more serious things."

Alfred smiled as he sat down to work on a petition for a new patent. This one would protect his method of using one charge to set off another — the revolutionary discovery of firing nitroglycerin by detonation which, scientists years later were to agree, changed the whole technique of explosives and "laid the foundations of the entire modern manufacture of explosives."

To Alfred's surprise, when he read the application

to his father it met with Immanuel Nobel's strong opposition. He did not object to the wording but to the fact that the application was in Alfred's name. The earlier patent had not seemed too important to the father, who remembered his own failure with the nitroglycerin mixture. He had encouraged Alfred to take that patent out in his name. Now, however, with the growing commercial importance of the new explosive, Immanuel Nobel insisted that his name be included on the patent.

For the first time, there was real and serious disagreement between father and son. Alfred insisted that he was entitled to control the rights of the invention since he had been chiefly responsible for it in the first place and had worked out the improvements that had made it salable.

To set forth his points without interruption or argument, Alfred wrote his father a letter. In it he went over, step by step, the history of the new explosive. He referred to his father's writing him in St. Petersburg that he had developed a powder twenty times more powerful than the old gunpowder and asking him to offer it to the Russian Army engineers.

Alfred mentioned his trip to Stockholm and their disappointment when his father's new explosive was tested. He referred to his own successful experiments after his return to St. Petersburg and the fact that they were halted by the second trip to Stockholm and the second failure in his father's claims. After wasting a whole summer trying to improve his father's invention, Alfred wrote, he had gone back to his own method, though his father had laughed at him for it. That principle, Alfred stated, was that "if a small amount of pyroglycerin (nitroglycerin) be rapidly caused to explode, the shock and the heat generated will communicate the explosion to the whole mass." And so, Alfred concluded, since this patent would be based on methods which he himself had invented and improved, he felt it clearly should be in his name.

Immanuel Nobel did not reply to his son's letter. Fru Nobel made excuses for him — he was accustomed to being the principal figure in anything of that sort; he was not feeling well. But she told Alfred that she was glad he had dealt firmly with the situation.

Not that it seemed to help much. Herre Nobel continued to sulk stubbornly. He quit going to the workshop and claimed that he had lost interest in the nitroglycerin explosive. He took most of his equipment home and began to work there again on his old love, the explosive mine. His talent in that field was beyond doubt; that summer he took out a patent on an improved mine.

Fru Nobel was deeply distressed by the rift between her husband and son. She tried her best to lessen it and to lighten the strained atmosphere in the usually harmonious home. When Emil came home for the long vacation he was careful not to take sides, but he promptly went to work with Alfred in the workshop-laboratory.

Alfred was glad to have the help of his young brother. Besides being genuinely fond of him, he respected Emil's ability in experimental chemistry. They had less time to work together in the laboratory than he wished. So many requests were coming in for Alfred Nobel to call at this office or that quarry or mine that he had to be away a great deal. The assistant was working out nicely; he and Emil got on well together. As orders increased, Alfred took on a maid and an errand boy to help with packing and delivering the orders. The Nobel workshop was getting to be quite a place!

Finances were still the problem. It cost money to buy chemicals and ingredients for the explosive and for experimental purposes. It cost money to meet the weekly payroll, even for so few employees. Immanuel Nobel stubbornly insisted on paying out of his meager funds the monthly rent for the workshop since he had arranged for it and it was taken in his name. Alfred rushed about, picking up small orders from mining and construction companies, putting on demonstrations, answering questions. Between times he worked with Emil and the assistant in the laboratory, intent on making the product more powerful and more uniformly dependable. The patent had been granted — in his name. He put the paper away carefully, saying nothing to his father about it.

Everyone in the Nobel household was pleased — even the father, though he took pains not to show it — when the Swedish Government became a customer for "Nobel's blasting oil." The railroads, owned and controlled by the government, were bringing the tracks from the south into the heart of Stockholm.

This involved tunneling through the cliffs which lay to the south of the city proper, and the engineers had ordered the new explosive for the blasting job. It would be something to turn out this big order in the little workshop, especially without Immanuel Nobel's help, but Alfred was confident it could be done.

Another cheerful note was the interest of a very wealthy Stockholm businessman in the young business. Herre Smitt was much impressed by the inquiries and orders coming in to Alfred Nobel every day. He could see a big future for a powerful explosive, what with all the industrial development going on and new railroads and highways being built. He advanced Alfred some badly needed money to take care of current needs and promised that in the fall they would get together and organize a real company. Alfred had an aunt to thank for this prospect, for it was one of his mother's sisters who had introduced him to Herre Smitt.

The third day of September, 1864, was the day when the two largest orders they had filled were to go out — fifty pounds of the explosive to the Ammeberg mine and two hundred and fifty pounds to the government engineer in charge of blasting the railroad tunnel. Alfred hated to be away, but he had to go out on one of his calls. The assistant and Emil would have to take care of the details connected with getting the two orders out.

Toward noon a breathless messenger found Alfred and summoned him home. The man's story was incoherent, but disaster was written all over his white face. The drive back to Heleneborg was agony to Alfred, though outwardly he remained calm. When they reached the neighborhood of the workshop he could see people crowding about. But where was the workshop? Then he saw — a mass of tumbled walls and smoking ruins! Firemen, police, and volunteer helpers swarmed about, as well as curious spectators. At the side, under sheets borrowed from a neighbor, was a row of bodies. Alfred's heart turned to ice.

Quickly he walked the short distance to the house, hoping unreasonably to find Emil there. When he saw his father rocking back and forth in speechless agony and his mother sitting beside him, motionless as a statue, Alfred knew the worst. He clasped his mother in his arms, took his father's hand for a second, and then, without a word, went back to the scene of the disaster and took over. Pale-faced, jaws set, seemingly calm, he assumed full responsibility for the factory and did all the grim things that had to be done. With the police making notes and asking questions, he identified the bodies, except for a fifth who must have been passing at the time of the explosion. He answered the queries of newsmen who had hurried there, sensing a sensational story. He listened to the reports of the neighbors — a terrific blast, a pillar of flame, collapsing walls, smoke.

The quiet gloom of a tragedy too deep for words descended upon the Nobel household. The quarrel between father and son was forgotten. Herre Nobel, overwhelmed, took to his bed. His wife hovered over him, bringing him food, which he rejected, and silent comfort, which he received gratefully. The relatives called and left, deeply depressed. Robert and Ludwig came home on brief visits and were appalled at the silent, heavy-hearted household.

Alfred found himself in the midst of legal and financial difficulties. It seemed that the Nobels had no license for manufacturing explosives for sale. Alfred explained to the police that he and his father had not thought of the workshop as a factory but chiefly as a laboratory and that they had only recently begun to fill orders for their product. This did not satisfy the police, any more than Alfred's repeated statement that the Nobels had not regarded the explosive as dangerous. Not dangerous when it had just blown up a building and killed five persons?

But Alfred was serious. Since childhood he had been in close contact with explosives, and he had never had any reason to doubt his father's words: "If you know what you're doing and keep your head, you're all right." He had never seen anything that would make him feel any differently about nitroglycerin mixtures than about other explosive substances. Rather less so, in fact, since nitroglycerin did not burn or explode easily.

How, in view of his statement that the explosive was not dangerous, did he explain the fatal explosion? the police asked sternly. And to this question, Alfred had no answer.

He lay awake nights trying to figure it out. What could have gone wrong? Was it hurry? Defective materials? Careless handling by the assistant or by Emil? Or, more likely, some experimental tests on Emil's part? Unshed tears burned Alfred's eyes as he pictured Emil eagerly poised over his laboratory equipment. He forced his mind away and tried to look ahead. What would happen now? He had put all his hopes, all his ambition into this work with explosives. His latest invention was successful; it was important. Through it he could make a valuable contribution to industrial progress. That meant that he would be playing a real part in helping in mankind's advance! He must go on. He *must!*

But how? It looked like a dead end. Their city license was gone. There was no money. And yet — Alfred's whole nature insisted that he go ahead with his work. He had found the thing he could do best — an important, significant thing. He was making his rightful place in life. Police or no police, money or no money, he determined that somehow he would go on. Emil would want it. So would their father, if only he were as he always had been.

The next day Immanuel Nobel called his son to his bedside. For the first time he discussed the tragedy.

He asked Alfred his opinion as to its cause, and Alfred said frankly that he did not know.

"That," said Immanuel Nobel, "will not satisfy the authorities. That will not open the way for you to go on, as you must do. I shall write the police a letter, and you will help me."

"But what can you say?" Alfred felt both pity and admiration for this father who looked so frail and broken against the white pillows, yet whose old determined spirit was still strong.

"We shall see," the father murmured. "I have a plan. Bring paper and pencil."

For hours the two talked together. They made notes, tore them up and made new ones. In spite of Fru Nobel's protests, they worked on until the father was exhausted and Alfred drooped with fatigue. For a while they rested, then they went at it again. At last they completed their "Memorandum to the Stockholm Police."

In it they made Emil, darling of the family, the scapegoat. They placed the blame for the explosion squarely on the shoulders of the overeager college boy turned loose in the laboratory. In a well-meant effort

77

"to simplify the method of producing explosive oil," they wrote, he must have failed to note the temperature of the nitroglycerin. In the normal process of manufacture, "there was really no possibility of risk," Immanuel Nobel was careful to state, "since nitroglycerin is harmless."

Let the police — or all the world — think them hardhearted in accusing the dead son and brother! Immanuel and Alfred knew that he would have understood and approved. It was their best chance of convincing the authorities that there was nothing essentially dangerous in their work, requiring it to be outlawed. It was the only way Immanuel Nobel could think of to win a chance for that work to go on.

But the authorities were not impressed by the "Memorandum." Already they had canceled the Nobels' laboratory permit. Now they hurried through a municipal ruling forbidding the manufacture of explosives anywhere within the city limits.

Feeling against the Nobels ran high in Stockholm. The newspapers played up the disaster, making Alfred and his father look like criminals. How dared these men risk others' lives as well as their own, the newspapers asked, by experimenting with this diabol-ical explosive stuff? The Nobels must have known they were outside the law or they would have applied for a license when they started to sell the explosive. And now the son who had survived the explosion which killed his brother — the one they were trying to put the blame on — was actually defending their invention and talking of his work as calmly as if it were a legitimate business!

Perhaps, Alfred thought wryly, they would have been even more abusive if they had not known that the product was being bought by the government for the railroad-tunnel project!

People in the neighborhood would have nothing more to do with the Nobels. The idea of their coming back from Russia to make this quiet community into a death zone! Let them leave Heleneborg and take their devilish experimenting somewhere else!

Only the three people most closely concerned re-alized the full meaning of that explosion. To them — particularly to Immanuel and Alfred Nobel, and most of all to Alfred — something more was involved than the heavy cost in kronor, or the loss of esteem in the eyes of the community, or even their grief over Emil's death. They were faced with a challenge which touched their inventor's pride and their scientist's vision. Alfred, more than his father, could foresee the important part his explosive could play in making a better life for people by doing almost impossible tasks in engineering projects. Should all this be stopped by people who did not understand what they were doing — because of an unexplained accident?

"It was just that — an accident," Alfred said. And he added slowly, "One cannot expect an explosive substance to come into general use without waste of life."

The authorities to whom he made this statement thought it was about the most hardhearted remark they had ever heard. But to Alfred it was the simple truth, which he was prepared to accept and for which he was willing to risk his own life. Patient, sorrowing Fru Nobel could sense his feeling; Immanuel Nobel could understand it.

A month after the tragedy Herre Nobel had a stroke. Almost completely paralyzed, he was forced to lie helplessly in bed. His wife waited on him constantly. Now everything fell squarely on Alfred's shoulders. All questions were referred to him, all decisions made by him. He did not hesitate. The future was uncertain. Yet, sure that it was his duty and his destiny to go on working with explosives, he was also sure that a way would open up. He would watch for that way, doing whatever he could to encourage its coming.

"Were you in Russia so long you've forgotten your way around Stockholm, Alfred?" Fru Nobel stopped by the table, tray in hand, and leaned gently over her son's shoulder.

Alfred barely looked up, he was so intent on the map he was studying. It was a map of Stockholm, full of the islands and jutting peninsulas and winding channels that lay between Lake Mälar and the sea. All this territory, including Heleneborg on the western end of the Södermalm peninsula, was banned as a location for an explosives factory. And such a factory was a necessity for the company Herre Smitt was ready to form.

Alfred ran his fingers along the line indicating the

city limit. To rent or buy a suitable piece of property beyond it would be out of the question with all the other expenses facing him. His forefinger rested on the irregularly shaped Lake Mälar. It, too, lay outside the city ban.

"Lake Mälar!" Alfred said aloud, and a light danced in his sober eyes.

The next few days were filled with rather unusual activities for Alfred Nobel. He rented an old barge anchored beside a little dock on the south side of Lake Mälar. Then he hired two carpenters to build on its deck as large a shed as the space would hold. With money advanced by Herre Smitt he bought chemicals and equipment and fitted up the shed as a workshop. And then he had the barge towed a little way out from shore and went to work in his floating factory.

The city authorities were indignant; the residents along the lake front were furious. They blustered and they threatened, but there was nothing they could do. Lake Mälar was outside the city ban, and Alfred Nobel was within his rights.

Rather to his surprise, he found a capable young

engineer willing to work with him on the barge. Together they began mixing the explosive oil. Now the
orders which had piled up could begin to be filled.
Now Alfred could talk business with Herre Smitt.

The fatal accident had made Herre Smitt all the
more eager to back up this persistent young man and
his explosive oil. Regretful though it was, the accident had certainly demonstrated the power of his product. And the more powerful the product, the greater
its commercial possibilities. The tragedy had impressed
others the same way. Hardly waiting a decent length
of time, they had sent in inquiries and orders from all
over the world.

In late October, the first company was formed to
handle the nitroglycerin explosive. Herre Smitt and a
Herre Wennerström put up the money; Alfred Nobel
contributed his Swedish patent rights and his skill. Of
the one hundred and twenty-five shares, the two investors took sixty-three and Alfred and his father —
for Alfred insisted on including him in the company
— the remaining sixty-two.

Now Alfred was more or less freed of money troubles, though after he had paid the costs of the tragic

explosion and of setting up the barge workshop, there was not a great deal left to go on. In addition, Alfred had taken over the financial responsibility for the Nobel household, including the expense of doctors and medicine for his father. But at least he was free now to devote himself to his work.

Free, but beset with difficulties. The lakeside residents raised such a fuss about the barge that every few days Alfred paid a man to tow it to some other location. He could see that this could not go on indefinitely. Besides, the lake breezes did not make the floating factory exactly the most comfortable winter working place. So, along with everything else, Alfred had to find time to explore the environs of Stockholm, looking for an "uninhabited locality." For this was the only sort of place where the authorities would permit an explosives factory to be built. Ten miles out, on the shore of Lake Mälar, he found what he was looking for at a price he felt the company could afford. That winter he supervised the construction of a simple factory to which they would move in the spring.

How he kept going during those months no one

knew, least of all himself. He worked with a fierceness that annoyed his enemies and worried his mother. He paid no attention to his health, to the violent headaches caused by the nitroglycerin, to the emotional strain he was under. He made tests, directed manufacture, gave demonstrations in mines and quarries, arranged sales, and kept the books.

In March, 1865, the little business moved from the raft to dry land. In the new factory at Vinterviken, Alfred Nobel started the world's first factory for the manufacture of a nitroglycerin explosive. Orders poured in. In spite of its rather high price, miners and engineers were finding the new explosive cheaper to use than human labor.

This rather high price was the cause of much concern to Alfred Nobel. The reason for it was that it took so much time to make any sizable amount of the explosive by the primitive process they used. They mixed nitric and sulfuric acids in exact quantities in great porcelain or cast-iron pots surrounded by cold water. Then, very slowly, they poured in the glycerin, constantly stirring the mixture with a glass rod. This generated considerable heat, so the mixture was allowed to stand for a few hours. When it had cooled and the oily nitroglycerin had settled to the bottom, they took it out and washed it with pure cold water.

Alfred knew that he must work out a better way to produce the oil in quantity. Then they could sell it for less. But before he did that, he realized that he must protect his rights to his invention by patenting it in other countries before someone else got ahead of him.

He sold his first foreign rights in the neighboring country of Norway, and he sold them outright so that he could give his parents money to go to a health resort. Immanuel Nobel had the idea that this would benefit him, and perhaps he was helped a little by the change. But his condition was not much improved, and he continued to be pitifully dependent on his wife. At the same time, his mind was active, and he spent much of his time figuring out new inventions.

More and more mines were now using the Nobel product. Many orders were coming in from Germany and Belgium. Robert had changed his mind about Alfred's invention and was going to give up his unprofitable lamp-and-oil business and start a nitroglycerin explosives factory in Finland. Herre Wennerström, the second investor in the Swedish company, went to Norway to see about setting up a factory there.

Alfred could see that the time for expansion had come. With things going well in the Swedish factory, he decided to have a try at Germany. So, in the spring of 1865, leaving the young engineer in charge of the Vinterviken plant, Alfred Nobel took off for the busy commercial city of Hamburg, Germany.

5

The
Way Up

THERE WERE GOOD REASONS for Alfred Nobel to choose
Hamburg as the place to begin his business expansion.
It was the largest seaport in Europe and one of the
liveliest trade centers. Ocean-going vessels steamed
from Hamburg down the Elbe River to the North Sea,
carrying passengers and freight direct to London, New
York, and other world ports.

One of the Swedish quarry owners who had been
using the Nobel blasting oil had a brother, Herr
Winkler, who was a big businessman in Hamburg, and
he was eager to start a nitroglycerin company in Germany. Soon after Alfred Nobel arrived, Herr Winkler
arranged for him to put on a demonstration of the new

explosive at a nearby race track. The demonstration went off so well that it brought a wealthy lawyer into the new company. The three partners — the Swedish inventor, Alfred Nobel, the Swedish-born German merchant, W. Winkler, and the German lawyer, Dr. Bandmann — organized the new German firm of Alfred Nobel & Co., registering it officially at the Hamburg city hall in June, 1865.

The company's first job was to fill the orders which had been coming in from Germany and nearby Belgium. Handling them in Hamburg would save time and expense over sending them on to the overcrowded Vinterviken factory in Sweden. A temporary workshop was set up in one of Herr Winkler's warehouses to prepare the explosive oil and ship it out.

The company's next job was to build a factory. The partners investigated various possibilities near Hamburg. Finally they decided to buy an old tannery at Krümmel, a small village a few miles farther up the Elbe River.

It would take several weeks to get the permit to build the explosives factory. Alfred Nobel left the details in the hands of Winkler and Bandmann and took this time to go to various European cities to try to interest governments and financiers in his invention. He went first to Vienna and then to Paris, but he did not succeed in stirring up interest in either place. This was disappointing. And yet it was encouraging to learn in Paris that the French Government had thought well enough of the nitroglycerin explosive to appoint a commission to investigate its military pos-sibilities. While he looked forward to industrial uses for nitroglycerin, Nobel was not going to discourage its use in any field. But there was not a thing he could do to influence the commission or to hurry it toward its decision.

In Turin, Alfred Nobel, the man who had made nitroglycerin practical and useful, met Ascanio Sobrero, the man who had discovered the substance in the first place. Professor Sobrero was a scientist, not an inventor. When he realized the powerful possi-bilities of the chemical he had produced, he was alarmed. He was perfectly willing to demonstrate the power of nitroglycerin by exploding a single drop of it with a red-hot needle, but beyond that he did not care to go. Still, he was pleased when the inventor who had developed something important from the substance called to pay his respects.

In November, Nobel went to London. Here, as in Vienna and Paris, he did not find anyone he could interest in his explosive. He went back to Hamburg feeling that his whole trip had been a failure.

There was good news in Hamburg. The factory permit had been granted; the building at Krümmel was started; orders were pouring in. Theodore Winkler, the Swedish quarry owner, had written his brother that he would like to come over and join them. By the time the Krümmel factory opened, there were four members of the firm. Theodore Winkler took over the selling end of the business and the partners engaged a German chemist to handle production. By now there were enough orders to keep not only the Krümmel factory busy but also the factories in Norway, Sweden, and Finland.

Robert Nobel, never fond of Finland, had been glad to turn over the Finnish factory to someone else and to become sales manager for the Swedish factory at Vinterviken. This had been Alfred's suggestion. He knew how delighted the old parents would be to have Robert and his wife and family near them. The father was a little better but far from well. Neither Ludwig nor Alfred could get home often. Ludwig's little machine shop in St. Petersburg had grown into a large factory for the manufacture of firearms, principally for the Russian Government, and he had settled there permanently.

The use of the nitroglycerin explosive was spreading. From the Krümmel factory it was being shipped practically everywhere — to Germany, Austria, Belgium, England, the United States, and even to faraway Australia.

In America, unscrupulous men were trying to get ahead of Nobel by claiming his invention and the right to handle the blasting oil in the United States. They meant to take advantage of the opportunities offered by the westward expansion of railroads, by the gold mining in California, and by the oil discoveries in Pennsylvania. One man, a Mr. Shaffner, was particularly clever and persistent in his attempts to outdo Nobel in America.

This Shaffner had already turned up on several occasions. He had gone to England to promote the Atlantic cable business there, and from England had gone on to Russia to act as a military adviser during the Crimean War. He claimed that while in St. Petersburg he had visited the Nobel plant and had, in fact, been present when the Nobels had experimented unsuccessfully with nitroglycerin. He succeeded in learning a good deal about the Nobel mines — knowledge which he made use of later in Denmark. At the time of the fatal explosion in Heleneborg, he was in Sweden, instructing the Army and Navy in the use of mines. Like many others, he was impressed by that explosion. Not by its tragedy but by its demonstration of the power of the new explosive the Nobels were working with. Sensing that they needed money, Shaffner went to Alfred Nobel and offered to buy from him the American rights to his invention. When Alfred refused to sell, Shaffner tried to get the United States minister to Sweden to secure information for him on the invention, which of course the minister refused to do.

Back in the United States, Shaffner demonstrated the mines he had learned about in Russia and had gone on working with. He succeeded in interesting General

Grant in using them in the War between the States. But he had not forgotten the nitroglycerin explosive oil. When, in the fall of 1865, he learned that Alfred Nobel's patent application for it was pending in Washington, Shaffner immediately applied for a patent in his own name. He claimed that he had made the nitroglycerin explosive ahead of Nobel.

Across the Atlantic, in Hamburg, Alfred Nobel heard of this and was furious. He contested Shaffner's claim. At the American consulates in Stockholm and in Hamburg, witnesses testified under oath to Nobel's much earlier use of the blasting oil. Miners from Ammeberg and men from Swedish quarries told of his early tests in Sweden. Shaffner lost his case but not his brazen courage. He had realized that he was taking a chance, counting on Nobel's being across the ocean and also on the vague terms of the Nobel patent application.

It was Nobel's second Swedish patent — the one which had caused the trouble with Immanuel Nobel — which Nobel had sent to a patent lawyer in Philadelphia as a basis for the American patent application. The original Swedish patent had not been very clear, and since the American lawyer did not understand the chemical principles involved, he had written a very inadequate description of the invention in the American patent application. Almost anyone who knew anything about explosives could find flaws in the patent and take advantage of it. Shaffner was the first to try to do so, but by no means the last.

Nobel did not have any definite ideas about handling his patent rights in America, but others did. At the time Dr. Bandmann joined the Nobel German firm, an American friend of his, by the name of "Colonel" Burstenbinder, happened to be in Hamburg. Burstenbinder saw the remarkable demonstration Nobel put on at the Hamburg race track and became so interested in the new explosive oil that he asked for samples to take back to America. He could think of all sorts of ways that such a powerful explosive could be used in America and could see a fortune for the person who introduced it there. The partners gave Burstenbinder samples of the new explosive and Nobel showed him how to demonstrate it.

A few months after Nobel's American patent was granted, Burstenbinder set up a stock company in the

United States to sell shares in the invention. Then — and not till then — he wrote Nobel, offering him a sum of money and a certain percentage of the shares in return for his American patent rights. Nobel was disturbed that this stock company had been set up without his knowledge or consent. He was not at all sure that he liked the idea.

There was still another American activity connected with the new explosive at this time. A brother of Dr. Bandmann's had an importing business in California, where he lived. This Julius Bandmann could see that there was a big market for the explosive oil in connection with the gold mining there. He proposed acting as an agent for Nobel & Co., which seemed like a good idea to all the partners in Hamburg. And so shipments started to go regularly from the Krümmel factory across the Atlantic to Panama, to be transported by land the short distance to the Pacific Ocean and then, by sea again, up the west coast of North America to San Francisco and Julius Bandmann's warehouses.

With all this American interest in nitroglycerin, Alfred Nobel decided that he should make a trip to the

United States. He wanted to investigate the matters of the faulty patent and of Burstenbinder's doubtful stock-company promotion. And he wanted to encourage and promote the widespread use of the blasting oil in America. But before he reached New York in late April, 1866, there had been another and more serious development in the nitroglycerin story.

Up to this time, no one had had any real idea of the dangers involved in handling nitroglycerin. Warned by the Heleneborg disaster, Nobel had tried to make its manufacture as safe as possible. But it was hard to make others be careful. As he said, "People get extremely careless when they have dealt for a little time with these explosives. For instance, a chemist who, the first time he makes nitroglycerin in large quantities, is almost frightened to death, a fortnight afterward gets so careless as to expose himself to the utmost danger."

Even so, it was easier to control carelessness in the manufacture of nitroglycerin than in its handling. Most people, including Alfred Nobel, thought the stuff was entirely harmless at almost all times and they took practically no precautions in handling it. The explosive oil was put into square zinc or tin cans, which were placed in wooden crates stuffed with shavings, sawdust, or dirt. If the nitroglycerin was not entirely pure, acids might eat holes in the can and let the milky-looking oil run out. Tin cans full of nitroglycerin were often carried on two-wheeled carts over rough roads. The stuff, jolted around, sometimes leaked out of the cans and trickled down over the wheels. More than once a workman mistook a can of nitroglycerin for grease and used it to oil the wheels of his cart or his boots or leather breeches. In winter the oil would freeze, and men would cut it up with blows of ice picks.

Herre Wennerström, partner in the Swedish firm, was surprised but not greatly alarmed when some bottled samples he was carrying to Norway fermented and the gases blew out the corks.

A Swedish army officer who had been making tests with Robert Nobel took two unused bottles of nitroglycerin with him when he rode home in a public coach. He put them in the rack on top of the coach and sat inside, laughing and joking with an amusing companion. He wrote that he thought nothing of it as he heard the bottles jounce and rattle overhead. One bottle broke and "the contents oozed over the side of the carriage and the wheels; the other, strangely enough, survived the coachman's hurling of the box from the top of the coach to the hard ground."

Robert Nobel wrote of taking a week-long bus trip, loaded with samples for use in demonstrating the explosive in southern Sweden. "The really extraordinary thing," he commented, "was that we did not blow ourselves into atoms fifty times a day."

It was really astonishing how long luck held, but this careless handling of the powerful explosive could hardly go on indefinitely without serious trouble. That winter of 1865 and the following spring there was a succession of unscheduled, fatal explosions.

In Silesia, a railroad worker was blown up when he tried to cut some frozen nitroglycerin with an ax.

In Westphalia, Germany, a miner "asked for two pounds of blasting oil. The clerk started to pour it out, and that was the last of the clerk, the miner, and the store."

A German who had brought to New York ten pounds of nitroglycerin in a flask packed in a box left it at his hotel, intending to return for it. The porter lugged the box about from one place to another. One day, noticing a red vapor coming from it, he hurriedly carried the box out into the street. A moment later there was a great explosion. Windows were broken, houses damaged, and a four-foot hole torn in the street.

In March, 1866, there was a bad explosion at Sydney, Australia, when two cases of nitroglycerin blew up a warehouse, killing no one knew how many persons.

The next month, while the steamer *European* was docked at a Panama port, seventy cases of nitroglycerin, bound for San Francisco, were being moved from the hold for their overland journey. Somehow they slipped out of the sling they were in. The steamer was blown up, together with somewhere between forty and sixty persons. The wharf and the freight houses next to it were completely wrecked, and a ship anchored nearby was damaged.

Two weeks later a driver drew up outside the San Francisco office of the Wells, Fargo Express Company. "The driver said 'Whoa!' and that was his farewell to life." Fourteen others were killed and all the buildings within the block collapsed in the tremendous blast.

News of the last few of these catastrophes met Alfred Nobel when he arrived in New York. He found that he was a very unpopular man. Hotels turned him away; people avoided him. There were rumors that he had brought cases of the "murderous compound" with him and stored them in a warehouse in the heart of the city. The fire chief had to investigate place after place to satisfy the frightened people. Reporters besieged Alfred Nobel for a statement. He told them that the accidents were due to careless handling and not to any danger inherent in the substance itself. He mentioned the number of shipments of nitroglycerin that had been made without accident. Then he announced that he would give a public demonstration to show the harmlessness of the blasting oil and just how it should be used.

Arrangements were made for the use of an abandoned quarry on Eighty-third Street in uptown Manhattan. Only about twenty men turned up. They stood at a distance as the small, quiet man placed a flat piece of iron on a big rock and poured onto it some explosive oil from a bottle. When he picked up a hammer and started to bring it down on the oil, the men rushed to the edges of the quarry. There was a short, sharp explosion. They looked back and saw that Mr. Nobel was standing only a little way from the rock, unharmed. He began to speak, and they came slowly back to hear what he had to say. They knew that he was Swedish, and they were surprised at his excellent English. He pointed to the puddle of oil still standing on the iron piece and explained that only the part hit by the hammer had exploded. The men backed off again as he lighted a match and set fire to the puddle; then they lingered to watch curiously as it burned but did not explode.

For two hours the Swedish inventor went through one test after another, finally using the percussion cap to set off a few good-sized blasts. At last the men started for home. They had come with fear, but they left with confidence. The stuff was harmless, they agreed, *provided* a person knew how to use it.

The quarry demonstration was duly reported in the papers, but it did not calm the public. Companies manufacturing and selling the old-fashioned gun-powder encouraged the people's fear. They did not want any new explosive to take the place of their product. City, state, and national legislative bodies held hearings to consider outlawing the explosive. In New York, Alfred Nobel testified at such a hearing. He repeated his belief in the harmlessness of nitro-glycerin; he was sure that all the accidents had been caused by careless handling.

Julius Bandmann wrote from California that he was up to his ears in trouble as a result of the accidental explosions. The city of San Francisco was putting through strict regulations about explosives. He had rebottled his stock of nitroglycerin in wine bottles, but even that did not throw people off the trail. No one would store the stuff. In desperation he had hired some Chinese laborers to put boxes of the bottles into a small boat and anchor it five miles out from shore, but he could not hope to leave them there long.

A few days later Bandmann wrote again. This time he had something else on his mind. He urged Mr. Nobel to come to San Francisco to help him intro-duce the nitroglycerin to gold-mining engineers. They were using thousands of pounds of gunpowder, he wrote, when the new explosive would serve their purpose much better and save them both time and money.

But Alfred Nobel did not go to San Francisco. Too many things were happening in New York. To his surprise, Mr. Shaffner came to call on him. Shaffner did not mention the patent business but breezily offered his help and advice in the difficult situation created by the accidental nitroglycerin explosions. "We explosives experts must stick together," he said. Under the circumstances, Alfred Nobel could hardly afford to make an enemy of the man by being unfriendly.

"Colonel" Burstenbinder was in a dither. He was being sued by the Wells, Fargo Express Company because the explosion which destroyed their San Francisco place had been traced to a shipment of nitroglycerin sent by him. Because of this, he could not take a cent of the money which financiers, intrigued by so much evidence of the power of the explosive, were eager to invest in his stock company. Burstenbinder had no notion of letting that money go to Wells, Fargo instead of into his pockets!

Alfred Nobel, seeing that Burstenbinder could not — or would not — act, decided that he had better get into financial matters himself. Otherwise he would never get from his American patent rights the same sort of money return that he had received from patent rights in other countries. A company was hastily formed, and in June, Nobel turned over his American patent rights to the New York-incorporated United States Blasting Oil Company, one of whose officials was none other than Mr. Shaffner!

Between business and legal appointments, demonstrations of the nitroglycerin explosive, and carrying on a large correspondence in several different languages, Alfred Nobel somehow found time to work on the problem of producing a safer product. He knew that he must make nitroglycerin less dangerous to transport and to store. He was appalled at the loss of life and property it had caused. Yet never for a moment did he lose his faith in his invention's importance to industry or his determination to go on with it.

Two more catastrophes, both of particular grief to Alfred Nobel, were added to the growing list. In May, the Krümmel factory blew up, and in June, the one in Norway. People everywhere now were terrified of the new explosive. From all sides appeals came to the inventor to stop making it. Why, they asked, had he ever unloosed this dreadful stuff on the world?

Theodore Winkler begged Nobel to return to Hamburg, bringing money if possible. It would, he wrote, need a good deal more of it than the German firm had to rebuild the Krümmel plant, put it on its feet again, and fight the wave of feeling against the new explosive. France and Belgium were considering prohibiting it altogether. Sweden, England, and some other countries were making strict regulations about its handling and transportation.

Nobel's American affairs were far from straightened out. He wanted to work out legal safeguards to protect the American patent rights. He wanted to see the United States Blasting Oil Company firmly established with a factory and permits to produce the explosive. He wanted to get an agreement between Bandmann in California and this new company to have the nitroglycerin for the West Coast supplied from the East Coast instead of from Germany. But all these things, he decided, were less important than for him to get back to Hamburg. So in July he left New York, taking with him the ten thousand dollars he had received for his American patent rights and twenty-five hundred shares in the United States Blasting Oil Company, minus one hundred and twenty-five which he gave to Burstenbinder.

In Hamburg, Nobel turned the money over to his partners to settle some of the company bills and headed for a laboratory. In the partly rebuilt Krümmel factory he set to work on the problem which faced him. There, day after day, he concentrated on his experiments to develop a safer nitroglycerin explosive.

His idea was to combine the nitroglycerin with a nonexplosive substance which would make it safer to handle and yet would not seriously lessen its effectiveness. At first he tried adding a nonexplosive liquid. Wood alcohol seemed a satisfactory solvent; it also prevented the nitroglycerin from freezing, which had been a problem. But how much better a solid substance would be than a liquid! In solid form nitroglycerin could be handled, transported, and stored far more easily and safely than as a liquid in bottles or cans. After much thought Nobel decided against a liquid in favor of a solid which would absorb the nitroglycerin. Powdered charcoal, he discovered, was good — but not good enough. Sawdust would work.

Nobel tried many substances before he finally hit upon the perfect one — kieselguhr. This was simply a porous clay, but it had all the necessary properties. It was light; it could be depended on to act the same way every time; and — most important — it was so absorbent that it would take three parts of nitroglycerin to one of itself. Another thing, it was available nearby in limitless quantity, and so was dirt cheap. And Nobel knew that near almost any factory there would be some kind of siliceous earth similar to kieselguhr.

Alfred Nobel proceeded with caution, putting the porous substance through all sorts of tests and comparing it with various other substances. When the nitroglycerin-kieselguhr mixture came through every test, Nobel knew that he had his finger on something big. He called the new substance dynamite, from the Greek word *dynamis*, meaning power or force. The factory workers insisted on calling it "Nobel's safety powder."

That fall the Krümmel factory began to manufacture dynamite. Early in 1867, the factory was ready to deliver it in quantity. For a while some customers stuck to the liquid nitroglycerin they were used to, in spite of its dangers and the many new government regulations, but before long they gave it up in favor of the new explosive. The solid form was so much safer to carry, easier to store, simpler to use!

Dynamite quickly grew in popularity. Soon the Krümmel factory stopped manufacturing the dangerous old nitroglycerin liquid entirely and produced nothing but the solid form — dynamite. The factories in Sweden, Norway, and Finland, too, changed over to the production of dynamite. Sales increased enormously, and money began to pour into Alfred Nobel's pockets.

Dynamite caught the popular fancy. The same people who had been almost hysterically fearful of nitroglycerin, the very people who had wanted it outlawed, now were all for this powerful yet safe explosive. They seemed suddenly to grasp the inventor's vision of its close-to-limitless possibilities in clearing land; in constructing roads, railroads, canals; in blasting tunnels — even under water; and for doing dozens of other great constructive jobs. Dynamite became indispensable. And almost overnight Alfred Nobel joined the ranks of the great inventors.

His earlier invention, known as the "Nobel lighter," did not lose its importance when dynamite replaced the liquid nitroglycerin. A fuse and a percussion cap containing fulminate of mercury remained the key to the practical use of the explosive. The same old principle of setting off a big explosion with a little one still held good.

As the use of dynamite spread, Nobel shrewdly undertook the building of more manufacturing plants. In Bohemia, a model dynamite factory was constructed not far from Prague. In California, Julius Bandmann helped form the Giant Powder Company.

So far, both nitroglycerin and dynamite had been used almost entirely for peaceful purposes. This was the way Alfred Nobel envisioned them. He was pleased with the very real contribution his inventions were making to the progress of industry and com-

merce. But now the Prussians were at war with France
and they began to investigate the wartime possibilities
of Nobel's dynamite. Soon the Prussian Army was
buying from the Krümmel plant great quantities of
the explosive. They used it to blow up French roads,
bridges, and fortifications. Then German engineers
figured out ways of putting dynamite in bombs. And
they began to use the dynamite bombs in crowded
enemy areas, with devastating results.

In France, there was a government monopoly on
explosives. No private individual was allowed to manufacture them. Alfred Nobel formed a sort of business
alliance with a French steel firm which had good connections with the government. The owner's son, Paul
Barbe, thought he could get permission either to import dynamite or to manufacture it in France, but he
could not. Not until the Germans started using dynamite so effectively; then the picture changed. Then
Paul Barbe was not only granted permission to build
a dynamite factory in southern France, but he was
urged to do so quickly.

Less than six months after the factory was built
and put into operation, the war ended, and France

was forced to sign a peace treaty with Germany. Then once again the French Government forbade the private manufacture of explosives, and the Nobel-Barbe dynamite factory was shut down. The military importance of dynamite, however, was not forgotten.

What Alfred Nobel thought of this first wartime use of dynamite, in the Franco-Prussian War, he never, apparently, said — certainly not in writing. Yet he must have been conscious of the fact that his invention was being used in ways completely opposed to the constructive purposes he had intended.

During most of this time, Nobel was in England, trying to get his product accepted there. He had gone to England several times with his nitroglycerin but had got nowhere with the authorities. There were two reasons for this: the English were never very cordial to outside enterprise or foreign companies, and they were extremely cautious about anything which seemed less than completely safe. After the run of accidents with the liquid explosive, they had passed a strict Nitroglycerin Act. This forbade the importation, transportation, or sale of nitroglycerin in any form. Exceptions, which could be made in individual cases, required the special consent of a high official.

Nobel tried to get permission to bring dynamite into England by showing the difference between it and the old liquid nitroglycerin. He demonstrated the use of dynamite in quarries and mines. Once he had a ten-pound case of dynamite placed on a pile of wood and burned. Another time he had the same amount thrown from a sixty-foot cliff. To the spectators' amazement there was no explosion either time. Nobel wrote articles about dynamite for the newspapers and read scientific papers on it before learned societies. But the British were slow to make exceptions in favor of the new product. It was several years before Nobel succeeded in getting licenses to bring dynamite into England, and still longer before it could be manufactured on British soil.

At last, in 1871, the British Dynamite Company was formed. It was well financed. Most of the investors were Scottish; they had been more cordial to the whole idea than the English. Nobel was to hold half the stock in exchange for his patents and for acting as "scientific director" for the new company. He chose the site for the factory with extreme care. It was to be located at Ardeer, a bleak spot on the Firth of Clyde, near Glasgow. He disliked the place personally, finding it dreary and depressing, but that made no difference in his thinking. He was not there to enjoy life; he was there to construct a plant and, as always, he was absorbed in his work.

It took two years to build the Ardeer dynamite plant. Alfred Nobel stayed on the spot most of that time. His engineer friend Alarik Liedbeck came from Vinterviken to help him. They and their helpers planned everything with the greatest scientific efficiency and with the utmost regard for safety. Buildings were scattered and protected with earth mounds about them; only a limited amount of the explosive was permitted in a building; workmen wore special uniforms, without any metal on them. So well was everything thought out at the start that there was never a really bad accident in what became the world's greatest dynamite plant, at Ardeer, Scotland.

Before the Scottish plant went into production, Alfred Nobel was called back to Stockholm by his father's death. It occurred eight years to the day after the explosion at Heleneborg which killed Emil. Immanuel Nobel had never recovered from that blow. Yet his mind was alert and he had continued to have a "positive urge" to produce original ideas. Some of these were practical and more were impractical; he could not always tell the difference between them. One really amazing inventive idea was the making of a product from wood waste — layers of it pressed together in a composition veneer — the basic idea for plywood. He published a little book on it, calling it "an attempt to create a new industry in order to check the emigration mania resulting from the present lack of employment." But he did not have the strength to carry his idea into action, and his sons were too busy with other things to turn aside to do it. Perhaps, too, they did not realize its importance.

Alfred had visited his parents whenever he could, which was not often. In 1868, he had been pleased for his father's sake when the Swedish Academy of Science had presented Immanuel and Alfred Nobel jointly with the Letterstedt Prize "for outstanding original work in the realm of art, literature or science or for important discoveries of practical value to mankind." The joint citation to father and son stated that the award was given "to the former for his services in connection with the use of nitroglycerin as an explosive in general, and to the latter more particularly for the discovery of dynamite." It was characteristic of them both that, given their choice between a medal and money, they had chosen the medal. They were alike in many ways, and Alfred would always be in his father's debt for many things.

Fru Nobel continued to live in Stockholm, writing often to her sons and hearing often from them. As long as she lived, Alfred sent her birthday and Christmas gifts and visited her at least once a year, usually on her birthday. At this time the other two sons also came to see her, and there was a real family party.

The French partner, Paul Barbe, proved to be a strong helper. He was a man three years younger than Nobel, capable and energetic, and with an exceptional business sense and gift for organization. Although the French dynamite factory was closed, Barbe's interest in the business continued. Like Nobel, he could see that this was the time for expansion. He encouraged Nobel to form new companies and build new plants. The two men traveled to Switzerland, Spain, Portugal, Italy, and Hungary, in each country setting up a company with local investors but always holding the controlling shares themselves. Seven factories were built within two years, each in a different country.

Paul Barbe went with Nobel to England. He also visited the German plant at Krümmel and met Mr. Nobel's partners there. Although very much a Frenchman, Barbe was by no means a narrow nationalist and he got on well with businessmen and scientists of other countries. Yet he could not begin to be the internationalist Alfred Nobel was, both by nature and experience. Childhood in Sweden; youth in Russia; two years of travel in a dozen different countries; at home in six languages — Swedish, Russian, English, German, French, and Italian — and in their literatures, particularly the first three; experienced in carrying on business dealings and correspondence with people of these nationalities and many more; long residence in Sweden, Russia, Germany, and France, many lengthy visits in England, and two journeys to the United

States. No wonder that Alfred Nobel was an internationalist!

To be sure, wherever he was, his work was his greatest interest. He was not at all intrigued by social life, though he enjoyed intellectual conversations with people whom he liked and respected, whether in the world of science, literature, or art. He was something of a philosopher — a thinker as well as an inventor-scientist — and an idealist. He was a great reader. In his limited leisure time, when he was not well enough to work, at the health resorts to which he went occasionally all his life, and when he was traveling, he read. In this way he kept up with the major literary events in Sweden, England, and Russia. He still held the thought of doing some writing himself, but his busy life crowded this out. And perhaps his familiarity with so many languages was a drawback instead of a help in fulfilling his writing ambition. For he did not feel enough at home in any one language to develop an acceptable literary style in it.

With the invention of dynamite had come fame; with the expansion of the dynamite business had come wealth. But fame and wealth were demanding. Many people wanted to become acquainted with this great inventor; many more wanted something from him — scientific advice, a position, money. Alfred Nobel was a conscientious man and in spite of his poor health and crowded days he spent hours seeing people and reading letters asking for help. He disliked the hurly-burly life he seemed forced to live — traveling from place to place, holding long legal conferences and business interviews. He wanted badly to spend less time on the business side of his work and more time in the laboratory. And he longed to live quietly in one place instead of shuttling about constantly on trains and boats all over Europe.

Paul Barbe convinced Alfred Nobel that he should buy a home and settle down in Paris. From this inter-national capital of the world he could easily keep in touch with his widespread business activities. In Paris he would find laboratories and resources for scientific research. In Paris too he could enjoy the company of stimulating people, including many whom he already knew from previous visits.

And so, in 1873, forty-year-old Alfred Nobel bought a large house in the fashionable district near Paris's famed Arch of Triumph. Here in this beautiful city he hoped to settle down and live the peaceful, productive life he craved so much.

6

"The Loneliest
Millionaire
on Earth"

ALFRED NOBEL's Paris house was a fine one. An
arched gateway led to an inner court, beyond which
were stables and gardens. In the house a wide hall-
way led to the large study and, farther on, to the
rooms for living and dining. Every room was richly
and tastefully furnished. The pictures which hung on
the walls were not always the same, for Nobel had
made an arrangement with an art dealer to exchange
them occasionally for others which he would select.
A conservatory filled with rare plants was the favorite
setting for after-dinner conversation, which might be
carried on in French, Swedish, or English, according
to the nationality of the guests being entertained.

When Alfred Nobel entertained, he did so in an almost royal manner. He was an excellent host, considerate and gracious — and rather formal. He did not invite his guests haphazardly, just to have company. He enjoyed the society of well-mannered, intellectual men and intelligent, cultured, and beautiful women. He liked good conversation — informed talk about writers in France and England, Sweden and Russia, or lively discussions on serious philosophical subjects. He was a good listener; he could also be a sparkling conversationalist, touching lightly on weighty matters and telling anecdotes in an amusing fashion.

But dinner parties were the exception, not the rule, in the big Nobel house. Much of the time the famous inventor lived a very simple life there alone, except for the servants. He had few close friends. About this, and about life in general, he was inclined to be a bit melancholy. As he became richer, the idea grew in his mind that people liked him for his money and for what he could do for them rather than for himself. Often, alas, he had reason for his sometimes oversuspicious ideas of people's motives.

One of Nobel's favorite rooms was his study. He

would sit there by the hour, reading in the latest scientific or literary magazines from all over Europe, or in some thoughtful book. The study walls were lined with books in many languages. There were not only scientific works but also the best of the literature of practically all the European countries. The large desk was strewn with papers, though in an orderly fashion. As Alfred Nobel became more important in the scientific and industrial worlds his correspondence increased. He had a small desk installed for a secretary, but his letters were in so many different languages and so many of them seemed to require his personal attention that the small desk was empty most of the time and Nobel calmly went on answering his letters himself. He wrote longhand, in French, Swedish, English, German, Italian, or Russian, as the case might be.

As quickly as possible each morning, Alfred Nobel finished the necessary desk work so that he could go into his laboratory. He had made two rooms on the ground floor, next to the study, into a modern, fully equipped laboratory, and had engaged a French chemist as his assistant. The young man, Georg Fehrenbach, was capable, faithful — he stayed with Nobel for eighteen years — and interested in the chemist-inventor's problems. But, industrious though he was, he was not half so enthusiastic or hard-working as his employer. Every day, except when he was away on business trips or in the Paris office attending important conferences, Alfred Nobel spent long hours in the laboratory. It was nothing unusual for him to work fourteen or more hours in a day. Rarely at one stretch, however, for the nitroglycerin he worked with still brought on severe headaches, and his weak back and stomach still gave him trouble. He would work as long as he could, then lie down for a while, perhaps on the couch in his study, and then, as soon as he felt able, return to his work in the laboratory.

Alfred Nobel never dropped any experiment that seemed promising. He would go back to it again and again, working with great patience and rare imagination. Sometimes when he was sleepless at night an idea would creep into his inventor brain. Then he would rush down to the laboratory in the middle of the night to start an experiment. Often he became so engrossed in what he was doing that he forgot to eat. Naturally his never-strong constitution suffered from all this abuse. But Alfred Nobel had grown accustomed to paying little attention to the way he felt.

One relaxation he really enjoyed. In the stables off the court were several thoroughbred horses. On pleasant days Nobel would have a pair of them hitched to his fine carriage and go driving. He might drive through the great park which stretched for wooded miles not far from his home, or down the broad, tree-lined avenues, or beside the sparkling Seine. Alfred Nobel came to love the beautiful city of Paris and to feel very much at home in it.

There was an active Swedish Club in Paris of which he was a member. He was a member, too, of the Engineers Society. And there was a Swedish church to which he contributed generously. Its pastor, who was his friend, sometimes brought to his attention some needy case. Alfred Nobel never refused to help. "Although I am frequently taken in," he wrote the pastor in answer to one such request, "I am always glad to be able to help honest and industrious people out of difficulties against which they are struggling in vain." And he went on to say that he was sending a thousand francs instead of the six hundred the pastor had suggested. "I know well," he wrote, "that insufficient help is almost the same as no help at all." The Golden Rule was his motto, and he sincerely tried to live up to it.

In order to have more time to spend in his study and laboratory, Alfred Nobel tried to pass on to others as many of his business responsibilities as he could. Once he wrote to his eldest nephew, Emanuel, "It is my rule never to do myself what another could do better, or at any rate, as well. Were I not to make this my rule I should long ago have been worn out in body and soul, and probably ruined as well, for if you try to do everything yourself in a very large concern, the result will be that nothing will be done properly."

With Paul Barbe, Alfred Nobel set up in Paris a scientific advisory board to co-ordinate the activities of his various dynamite companies in different countries. He chose Alarik Liedbeck, the brilliant young Swedish engineer who had been at the Vinterviken plant, at Ardeer, and then at Krümmel, and his good friend, to head the board. After study, some changes were made not only in technical procedures but also in management and policy. Alfred Nobel stood aside from all the readjustment as much as possible, taking part only when an important decision was to be made.

Paul Barbe had finally succeeded in getting the French Government's permission to reopen the French dynamite factory. Now he and Nobel organized a French company, and this was incorporated, together with the older Alfred Nobel & Co., into an over-all company in which the Hamburg partners had their share.

There was no doubt that Nobel had a talent for business affairs. His reasoning was practical, his decisions sound. Time and again it was his quiet voice that turned the tide in favor of something which added to the stability or the development or the increased value of his almost world-wide business interests. Yet, unlike his partner Paul Barbe, he did not especially desire either power or money. Neither did he want fame. He would not be interviewed or have his picture in the paper, or even allow his name to be included in a book of famous Swedes. "I have no taste," he said, "for the buzz of notoriety." The driving forces in his life were his interest in science, his desire for industrial progress, his compelling urge to invent and perfect his inventions.

At this time the problem which filled Nobel's mind was the making of an explosive more powerful than dynamite and just as safe. When the liquid nitroglycerin was put in solid form, the inert kieselguhr absorbed some of the heat generated by the interaction of the acids. This lessened the pressure of the gases and cut down the power of the explosion.

In California, some miners were using dynamites with an "active" base — a product which combined the liquid nitroglycerin with an explosive solid substance. Nobel had deliberately turned his back on this possibility. Safety was his first thought when he chose the inert, porous kieselguhr as the solid absorbent for nitroglycerin. The Giant Powder Company in California, handling the Nobel dynamite, had much competition from the companies which sold the "active dope" dynamites. The Giant Powder Company wanted the courts to rule that the "active dope" dynamites were illegal, and they figured they would do this if Nobel would get American protection on his earliest nitroglycerin patent. But this he would not do, as he still would not sign himself "sole inventor" of that first nitroglycerin explosive which his father and younger brother had worked on with him. Neither would he do what the competing companies were doing and substitute an active, or explosive, substance for kieselguhr and so make the product less safe to handle and to use than dynamite. The answer, he decided, was to invent an explosive which would be as powerful as the "active dope" dynamites and as safe as the kieselguhr dynamite.

One day Nobel cut his finger. He put some collodion on it, but that night the finger continued to pain him. As he lay awake, he thought about the dynamite problem. He had tried adding nitrocellulose, or guncotton, to the nitroglycerin, but it made too dangerous and uncertain an explosive. Now, prompted by the aching finger and the collodion odor, he began to wonder how a small amount of nitrocellulose dissolved in ether alcohol (which was the basis of the collodion) would act. It was four o'clock. He got up, went down to the laboratory, and set to work. By the time Georg Fehrenbach arrived, the first specimen of a new form of explosive was ready. Because of its jellylike consistency, its inventor called it "blasting gelatin." There was much to be done to perfect it, but the idea was right.

Together, Alfred Nobel and his assistant made more than two hundred and fifty tests. They tried out different kinds of cellulose — the cell walls of plants, usually cotton — and different amounts of acids — sulfuric and nitric. They worked on various combinations and proportions of guncotton — the explosive made of nitrated cotton waste — and ether — the distillation of alcohol with sulfuric acid. When they had it the way the inventor thought it should be, the dynamite factories took over the testing, doing it on a larger scale. After they had proved that the blasting gelatin was practical to manufacture as well as effective to use, mechanics started designing new apparatus to make it in quantity. Then lawyers wrote up the patent applications for different countries. At last, that year of 1875, the manufacture and sale of blasting gelatin began.

It was an immediate success because of its many advantages. One was that it could be made in different strengths by using more or less of the cellulose. In this way, it could be made exactly right to fit the requirements of any situation. Another advantage was its suitability for use under water. An even greater advantage was its safety. But what engineers liked best of all was its terrific power.

One of the first big tests to which the gelatin dynamite was put was in blasting the nine-mile St. Gotthard tunnel under the Alps. Blasting gelatin was the ideal explosive for tunneling through the great rocky mountains in this pass connecting Switzerland and Italy. With dynamite, experts said, the cost of digging the tunnel would have been five million dollars more and it would have taken many more years than with the blasting gelatin.

In England the authorities, concerned as always with safety, tested Nobel's new explosive in various ways. They read with interest the news of its use in other countries, but they were determined to go slowly on its adoption in England, just as they had done with dynamite. They invited Alfred Nobel to speak on his subject at the Society of Arts in London. He traced the history of explosives and went into detail on the services of gunpowder — the old "black powder" which had been known and used for centuries. "Like a servant for all work," Nobel said, "it lacks perfection in each department, and modern science armed with better tools is gradually encroaching on its old domain." But he did not convert the English authorities to blasting gelatin; they did not allow it to be manufactured and sold in England until 1884, nine years after it was invented.

Elsewhere, the gelatin dynamite — later called "the legitimate parent of the war-celebrated TNT" — was taken up quickly. The invention added still more to Alfred Nobel's fame — and fortune. It also added to his burdens. When he had finished with the many details connected with testing, improving, and producing the new explosive, there were the legal steps involved in protecting the invention by patent in different countries. And then came all the business arrangements for the sale of the new explosive. Once more Nobel found himself spending most of his time with lawyers and in business conferences instead of in the laboratory. In addition, he was frequently invited to address various learned societies in European countries and to write papers for various scientific magazines in different languages. His already heavy correspondence grew still larger. Often he would write thirty or forty letters in a single day, switching from French to Swedish or English or German or Russian, as each case required.

In every batch of mail were requests for help. Most of these Alfred Nobel would not turn down without investigation. He was particularly generous to his own countrymen, and the Swedish colony in Paris came to depend on his support for many of its activities. He was also generous with young people, especially those who showed some leaning toward science. He would not only give them money and advice, but would arrange for them to go to school or to work in some special laboratory.

The quiet life Alfred Nobel had looked forward to living in Paris, centered in his study and laboratory, seemed to grow harder rather than easier to achieve. Clearly he needed help. Help in his correspondence, help in interviewing some of the many people who came to see him, help in entertaining the increasingly important guests he invited to his home. In spite of plenty of servants, including an excellent butler and a superb cook, the big house seemed empty. It lacked a woman's touch.

Alfred Nobel thought long and seriously about this. He had always avoided marriage because of his poor health, his absorption in his work, and his constant traveling from city to city and country to country. Perhaps he was influenced too by the love affair which, according to his poem, he had had in his youth. And perhaps he unconsciously compared every woman he met — unfavorably — with his mother, to whom he was deeply devoted. Although he could meet people easily and be very charming to them, he was really a shy man. In his own mind he belittled himself, thinking of himself as unattractive, though he really was not. As he grew older — and richer — he became convinced that any woman who would consent to marry him would do so only for his money. With his men friends he joked about remaining a bachelor. He made cynical remarks about women — especially Paris women — and said he never could find one he could get along with or who could get along with him. Yet women found him a pleasant and gallant companion, and he enjoyed their company.

Dismissing marriage from his mind, the lonely man wondered if he might be able to find a mature, cultured woman to run his household, act as his hostess, and help him with some of his correspondence. She must be attractive and capable, for she would be a sort of personal, confidential secretary. He would give her a suite in a wing of the big house and he would guard against the arrangement seeming in any way romantic. It would be best, he decided, for her not to be a Frenchwoman.

And so, with great care and caution, Alfred Nobel composed this advertisement and ran it in the Vienna *Presse:* "A rich, cultured, elderly gentleman, living in Paris, desires to find a mature lady, familiar with languages, to act as secretary and manager of his household."

In Vienna, the ad was read by a very unusual young woman in a very unusual situation. Bertha Kinsky was the only daughter in a noble Austrian family made poor by the father's early death and the mother's utter lack of money sense. After some rather ridiculous attempts to retrieve the family fortune and several disastrous romances, the beautiful Countess

Bertha Kinsky was engaged as governess for the four teen-aged daughters of Baron and Baroness von Suttner. In the von Suttner household Bertha fell in love with the girls' older brother — and he fell in love with her. The fact that Artur von Suttner was several years younger than she made no difference to either of them. But that, and the Kinsky family's financial plight, made considerable difference to the baron and baroness. They had no notion of letting this romance flourish. Neither, in her saner moments, did Bertha. She decided to run away from it, and she appealed to the baroness to help her find another position — the farther off it was from Vienna, she said, the better it would be.

The baroness saw the unusual ad in the Vienna paper and showed it to the governess. Although she did not really qualify for the job, for she knew nothing about either secretarial work or managing a house, Bertha answered the unsigned advertisement. Alfred Nobel's signature on the reply did not mean a thing to her, or to the baroness. But when the baroness inquired, she had no trouble in discovering that it belonged to a deeply respected and extremely wealthy inventor-industrialist in his early forties — not exactly "elderly"!

The prospective employer and employee exchanged several letters, and Bertha was engaged for the position. Whatever Alfred Nobel thought of her qualifications or lack of them, he must have been pleased at the prospect of having a well-born, well-educated lady in the lonely house. In her turn, Bertha was glad to find a well-paid position in Paris, a city she knew and liked, and this opportunity to forget at a distance her senseless romance.

Instead of sending someone to meet Countess Bertha Kinsky at the station, Alfred Nobel went himself, although the train arrived early in the morning. The suite he was having prepared for her was not yet ready — he was having the rooms completely redecorated and refurnished. And so he had engaged a suite in one of the best Paris hotels for her to stay in until everything was in readiness at the house. At the station he greeted the attractive young woman cordially and escorted her to her hotel. There he left her, promising to return for lunch.

As she unpacked and rested, Bertha thought about

this man who was going to be her employer. At forty-three, he was "a little below the medium height, with dark, full beard, with features neither ugly nor handsome; his expression rather gloomy, softened by kindly blue eyes."

When they met for luncheon in the hotel dining room, neither of them felt that the other was a stranger. They got along famously together; their conversation was lively and pleasant. That afternoon Alfred Nobel took the newcomer for a drive around Paris and then to his home. He showed her all over the place, paying particular attention to the rooms she would occupy.

For a week Alfred Nobel called on Countess Bertha Kinsky at the hotel every day. Their conversation ranged from practical talk about the ways in which she could help him to discussions of literary figures and philosophical ideas. One day he brought her the long poem he had written when he was a young man and let her read it. Years later she wrote that Nobel then left on her "the impression of a thinker and a poet, a man at the same time embittered and kind, unhappy and joyous, with unusual impulses and with a mistrust of man, passionately loving the great horizons of thought and profoundly despising human pettiness and stupidity, understanding everything and hoping for nothing." Mr. Nobel, she said, could tell a story so entertainingly that it captivated her completely. And he could converse on serious subjects in an equally agreeable and impressive way. Their conversations she found "an intense intellectual enjoyment."

But Alfred Nobel had other things to do besides entertain his new hostess. And in the hours when she was alone, Bertha Kinsky thought of nothing but her own misery. She was homesick and heartsick. Every day she heard from Artur and also from his young sisters. They wrote their former governess that Artur hardly spoke, he was so sad. So what else could Bertha do but sit down and write him a long letter, describing all her tender feelings toward him?

One day, noticing her melancholy, absent-minded manner, Alfred Nobel asked her suddenly, "Is your heart free?"

"No," Bertha answered honestly, "it is not." And when he encouraged her, she told him of her love for the young baron and of its hopelessness.

She had been brave to leave Vienna, Alfred Nobel told her. "Now be completely courageous," he advised. "Break off the correspondence also. Then let a little time pass . . . a new life, new impressions — and you will both forget — he perhaps even sooner than you!"

To take her mind off herself, Nobel told her of some of the inventions he was working on and of things he would like to do. He said that he wished he could produce a substance or a machine that would be so totally destructive that it would make war entirely unthinkable because it would be so horrible. Bertha remembered this later, but at the time she was so wrapped up in her own misery that she paid little attention to Nobel's astonishing ambition.

At the end of the first week, before the redecorated rooms were quite ready, Alfred Nobel had to go to Sweden for the opening of a new dynamite factory. The next few days were lonely ones for Bertha. Her mind and heart were still full of Artur. She sat in her room for hours at a time, brooding about her troubles. She had come to depend more than she realized on Nobel's daily visits, and she missed them. One day in the middle of the week she received two telegrams. One was from Sweden, from Alfred Nobel. He had wired to tell her of his safe arrival in Stockholm and of his intention to be back in Paris in a week's time. The other telegram was from Artur von Suttner. He had wired: I CANNOT LIVE WITHOUT YOU.

In a frenzy of excitement Bertha decided to defy the baroness, return to Vienna, and marry her true love. What if she was older, had no money, was disapproved of by his parents? Nothing mattered but love! She sold the one costly piece of jewelry she still had — a diamond cross. With the money she got for it, she paid her hotel bill and bought a return ticket to Vienna. Then, after writing a brief explanatory letter to Alfred Nobel, she went to the station alone and boarded the first train for Austria. In Vienna, Bertha Kinsky and Artur von Suttner were happily reunited and secretly married. They fled to the Caucasus in southern Russia, where Bertha had an influential friend who had long before invited her to visit there. This friend, Bertha was sure, would help Artur and her — the new Baron and Baroness von Suttner.

Alfred Nobel came back to his lonely house. He

closed off the unused, newly decorated suite intended
for Countess Bertha Kinsky. He never talked about his
disappointment in this relationship which had begun so
hopefully. Nor did he ever reproach Bertha for causing him considerable inconvenience and expense and
for giving him still another reason to distrust women.

For several years after Bertha Kinsky's entrance
into, and speedy exit from, Alfred Nobel's life, the
inventor did not produce any scientific idea which he
considered worth patenting. He had many business
affairs to attend to; he made occasional trips to Sweden, to Germany, to Austria, and to England; he spent
a great deal of time in his laboratory and in his study.
To the many invitations he received he usually replied
with a courteous "I regret."

As always, most of his energy and time was devoted to his scientific exploration. He found it difficult to do all the experiments he wanted to in his small,
though fully equipped, home laboratory. And so, in
1881, he bought a piece of land in Sévran, on the out-
skirts of Paris, and built there a larger, more modern
laboratory. He installed Georg Fehrenbach, his chem-
ist-assistant in Sévran and every day drove out to su-

pervise experiments and to work for hours on new ideas. Life might not hold for him what he wanted most — affection, health, and contentment — but so long as he could fill his hours with scientific work of importance he could not be completely unhappy.

7

The
Baku
Oil Wells

THE THREE NOBEL BROTHERS — Robert, Ludwig, and
Alfred — remained close to one another as they grew
older, in spite of distance and separate interests. The
mother in Stockholm was one bond; their common
childhood memories were another. They talked the
same language — though Alfred lived in France, Ludwig in Russia, and Robert in Sweden — for all of
them had inherited from the father a gift for mechanics and invention; all of them thought in broad terms,
looking toward the future and beyond their immediate
surroundings; and all of them were continually and
enthusiastically tackling new things.

Ludwig's machine shop in St. Petersburg grew by

leaps and bounds, for Ludwig Nobel was an excellent mechanical engineer, a good businessman, and a hard worker. Besides making all kinds of machine tools for civilians, he was soon specializing in firearms for the Russian Army, most of them made to its specifications and on its order. He modernized the Army's old-fashioned rifles and then contracted to supply it with new ones. For this, he took over an army arsenal and turned the place into a model factory.

Robert decided there was more future for him working with Ludwig in his firearms factory than staying with the Swedish explosives plant at Vinterviken. And so he and his family left Sweden and moved back to Russia. There he quickly learned Ludwig's business and became a great help to him.

It was difficult to get good hardwood for the gunstocks of the new rifles. Ludwig asked Robert to go to southern Russia to look into the possibility of using lumber from the great hardwood forests there. And so, in 1873, Robert took off on a lengthy trip into the Russian interior. He went from Moscow all the way south to the Caucasus Mountains, which span the broad strip of land between the Black and Caspian seas. He found plenty of fine walnut trees, which would have made excellent rifle butts, but they were in scattered places. Cutting and transporting them the more than twelve hundred miles north to St. Petersburg would make the project too costly.

At Baku, largest port on the landlocked Caspian Sea, Robert Nobel walked about the historic old town with its fascinating Persian mosques and ancient walls. He went to look at the "burning springs," where rich petroleum deposits bubbled up among the rocks. These springs had been known for centuries as one of the wonders of that part of the world. Some effort had recently been made to extract the oil and refine it for commercial use, but this had not been very successful. Robert learned that the government monopoly on these petroleum wells had expired only the year before. He had not been in the lamp-and-oil business in Finland for nothing. He knew the great and increasing demand for lighting oil. He knew that in the last ten years tremendous quantities of it had been exported from Pennsylvania, in the United States, for sale in all countries of Europe. America controlled the world market. But what an opportunity for someone here at Baku! The crudeness of the Baku petroleum did not bother him, for he was a good chemist and knew a thing or two about refining oil.

Back in St. Petersburg, Robert advised his brother against importing lumber from the Caucasus. Then he painted a glowing picture of the fortune to be made by going into the oil business in Baku. Ludwig was impressed by Robert's findings and by his enthusiasm, but he felt that he was not a good judge of the merits of the idea as he knew nothing about oil. He wrote Alfred about Robert's plan. Since both Alfred and he had done better financially than Robert, he said that he would like to give Robert a hand with this thing which appealed to him so much.

Without at all foreseeing the benefit to himself, Ludwig staked his brother to another trip to Baku and to the purchase of a small refinery there. Together they secured from the Russian Government the right to take over the Baku oil wells on a royalty basis.

In Baku, Robert set to work to modernize the methods that had been in use. Instead of hauling up the petroleum by hand in leather baskets from shallow, hand-dug pits, he installed drilling machinery imported from America. Instead of carting the oil in barrels on two-wheeled carts over six rough miles from the oil wells to the refinery, he put in a pipeline. There was trouble with the natives, who did not welcome change. For a time he had to hire men to stand guard over the pipes. But soon the local men saw that though they lost one job they might get a better one with the new company. Robert Nobel was a fair employer, and he was so in love with his work and did it with such skill and enthusiasm that he made progress against all odds.

It was exactly the right field for him. In Baku he could use his chemical training, the practical knowledge of oil he had gained in Finland, and his talent for detail and organization. His enormous faith in the future of the oil industry in general and the Baku business in particular was contagious. Soon not only Ludwig but young Emanuel became enthusiastic too.

There was clearly quite enough for one man to do handling the technical end of the business on the ground at Baku. So Ludwig agreed to take over the commercial side of things in St. Petersburg. To his surprise and pleasure, almost within months the project was paying off. Robert drilled new oil wells and doubled the length of the pipeline to reach them. He built larger refineries and storage tanks. Then he attacked the hardest problem, that of transporting the refined oil to market centers. He asked Ludwig to come down to Baku to see what he had accomplished and to help him solve the difficulties which remained.

Before Ludwig went to the Caucasus, he wrote to Alfred, urging him to go too. If the Baku oil venture should prove to be as big a thing as Robert thought, Ludwig wanted it to be a family affair, with Alfred in it too.

But Alfred could not get excited about oil. He thought he had enough irons in the fire already. He was glad that Robert was making such a success, and glad, too, that Ludwig was thinking of taking a trip. Instead of — or in addition to — going to Baku why not come to Paris? He would be delighted to have Ludwig visit him; they could talk over many things, including this oil business. As for his going to Baku, that was out of the question. He must go to England soon, and besides, southern Russia did not appeal to him at all, except to see Robert.

Ludwig decided to go to Paris. Perhaps a face-to-face talk would convince Alfred, as letters had not done, of the importance of the Baku oil project. Besides, Ludwig had some financial interest in Alfred's dynamite company and he wanted to discuss that, too. Most of all, it would be good to visit again with this younger brother of whom he was so fond and whom he had not seen for some time.

Ludwig took with him facts and figures about the Baku oil production. He showed Alfred that Robert was getting twice as much oil from the same amount of ground as he had been able to get at first, and that his refineries were upgrading the crude Baku oil to a level equal to that of American oil. Already it was competing with American oil in the European market.

Alfred was impressed. He agreed to put money into the project, though he said he had no time to take part in it actively. The Russo-Turkish War going on just then would prevent their forming a company at the moment, but the brothers agreed that as soon as the war ended they would incorporate the Baku oil business as a family venture.

Between business talks, Alfred entertained Ludwig

royally. He drove him about the city, took him to the Swedish Club and the Engineers Club. Best of all, they sat for hours in the big study, talking lovingly of their mother, laughing about childhood adventures they had shared, and sighing at the memory of old Immanuel and young Emil. They were both sorry when the few days' visit ended.

"Come on to St. Petersburg when you make your next trip to Stockholm," Ludwig urged. "Edla and I will be delighted to have you. We haven't as fine a house as yours here, but it is very comfortable. And you must see Emanuel. Eighteen this year, and almost as smart as his uncle!"

Alfred laughed. "If Emanuel is as nice and as bright a young fellow as he was a little boy, I'm bound to like him. I'll try to come, Ludwig."

The Russo-Turkish War ended within a few months, and in 1878, the Nobel Brothers' Naphtha Company was formed. Besides the three brothers, Ludwig's St. Petersburg factory partner was included in the corporation. He handled much of the commercial business in north Russia while Ludwig spent an increasing amount of time in the south. Robert's health was beginning to break under the strain of his hard work in the uncertain Caucasian climate. He spent a long vacation in Sweden and came back improved. But soon he was in poor health again, and the doctors advised him against living in the Caucasus. He took their advice, though he was distressed to leave the place he had developed beyond recognition. He bought an estate in northern Sweden and went there with his family to live. There were no money worries; the few brief years in the oil business had given Robert Nobel enough to live on comfortably for the rest of his life.

Robert had given his best to the Baku oil development, and it was very good. He had turned the crude little petroleum works on the shores of the Caspian into a giant industry using the best mechanical equipment and modern production methods. Now came Ludwig, with his quite different but equally valuable talent. "Success," he liked to say, "depends on vision, perseverance, industry, and thrift." Besides having every one of these virtues in large measure, Ludwig Nobel also had great ability for management and commercial expansion.

The year after the company was formed, Robert and Ludwig employed a Swedish shipbuilder to make a ship especially designed to carry oil. Instead of shipping oil in barrels on hired vessels, Nobel Brothers would own their own fleet of oil tankers. And they did. First one, then twelve, then four times that number. It has been said that "next to high explosives, the serviceable oil tanker is the most far-reaching achievement which the world owes to the Nobels." To get to Baku, these ships traveled the inland route from the North Sea to the Caspian, via the Neva River and several lakes and canals to the Volga and all the way down that mighty river to the sea. Then back again, loaded with oil.

In addition to the ships, Robert and then Ludwig invested in hundreds of specially designed tank cars which ran on the Russian railroads. They carried the Nobel oil to every city and town in the vast empire. At transfer points, huge storage tanks were constructed, following the American pattern. Through Ludwig's sound commercial instinct, oil in various grades and weights was made popular all over Russia. In peasant huts kerosene lamps took the place of the dangerous old wooden torches. Naphtha and gasoline became familiar industrial equipment.

It was difficult to induce capable technicians, chemists, and engineers to come to Baku and to stay there. The climate was variable, with violent winds blowing down from the frigid north in winter and sultry heat seeping up from the tropical south in summer. Vegetation was sparse; life was primitive.

So Ludwig Nobel became a housing-project pioneer. He embarked on an altogether new sort of enterprise. On a peninsula that jutted into the sea he built up a little village of homes for his "white-collar" workers. Grassy soil was brought in to landscape it and trees to give it shade. Someone who saw the place "before" and "after" said of Ludwig Nobel, "He created an oasis at cheerless Baku." There was a clubhouse with library and rooms for conversation and meetings and recreation. There were bowling alleys and tennis courts. More important, there were hospitals, and schools for the children, with teachers to run them.

In still another way Ludwig Nobel was a pioneer. He started a profit-sharing plan for the five thousand workers in the Nobel petroleum plant. Not even in progressive America had anything quite so forward-looking as this been done. And, long before it happened in Great Britain or in America, child labor was banned in the Nobel Brothers' Naphtha Company at Baku.

As the Baku plant grew, Alfred Nobel became more and more interested in it. In spite of himself, some of Robert's and Ludwig's enthusiasm rubbed off on him. Although he had said that he had no time to give to it, he began to think of possible improvements in methods and equipment. He dreamed of extending the pipelines the whole distance across the Caucasus, from the Caspian to the Black Sea. Then a fleet of ships waiting on the Black Sea could take the oil to northern ports via the Mediterranean, instead of steaming from the Caspian Sea the long winding way up the Volga. The sea route would also avoid the months of interruption in winter, when long stretches of the northern Volga were solidly frozen.

The pipeline from the Caspian to the Black Sea was never laid, but from an engineering standpoint it was a practical dream. Alfred contributed more realistically by working out better ways of evaporating the oil and of concentrating it. And he devised a system for the continuous distillation of naphtha, for which he obtained a French patent.

Most of all, however, Alfred Nobel helped with his money. Like Ludwig, he was surprised and pleased when he realized that Baku oil was a sound financial investment. In a few years' time it was earning millions, not only for the partners but for the Russian Government. Over a long period of time one sixth of all Russian revenues, it was said, came from the Nobel brothers' activities. The credit of the Nobel Brothers' Naphtha Company was good everywhere. Alfred Nobel kept putting in more money. He financed the technical improvements and ways of using by-products that Ludwig thought up, and he put up collateral for credit loans for the expansion Ludwig was so keen about. This tendency of Ludwig's worried Alfred. He remembered very well what had happened to their father in Russia years before. "You build first and then look about for the wherewithal," he scolded Ludwig. He preferred to work the opposite way.

As industrial concerns saw the Nobel oil interests prosper, competition sprang up. The wealthy Rothschild family began to buy up rival refineries in Baku. For a time, the Nobel Brothers' Naphtha Company was hard pressed. Ludwig's policy of borrowing heavily for expansion did not leave large money reserves. It was a question how long the company could stand the competitive price-cutting. The Rothschilds tried to block the Nobels' sources of credit in England and France. Then Alfred saved the day by standing in back of a bond issue in Germany. At this, the Rothschilds gave up their effort to put the Nobel company out of business. They even joined the Nobels and the Standard Oil Company in a cooperative scheme for distributing oil in western Europe.

Ludwig had wanted to hold the business closely within the family. Alfred, on the other hand, strongly favored wide ownership. Because of his feeling about this and because he was buying much of the stock, the 1883 stock issue was opened to the public. Ludwig regretted this and reminded Alfred that now they "must begin to observe formalities." And because of Alfred's greater experience with stock-company organization, Ludwig volunteered to follow his "advice and suggestions." Alfred was elected to the board of stockholders, but he had no desire to add to his business burdens. He soon resigned, content to leave as much authority as possible in Ludwig's hands.

This same year Alfred paid the return visit to St. Petersburg which Ludwig had urged. It was the first time he had been back since he left there as a young man. Many things had changed. The city had grown, and there were more foreigners than ever in it. Ludwig had become one of the richest and most important businessmen in all Russia. The family home was a pleasant one, with all the marks of convenient, cultured living.

The family could not do enough for Alfred's comfort and happiness. Ludwig, like Alfred, was a great reader and fond of thoughtful conversation. The two talked by the hour of things far removed from dynamite and firearms and the flourishing Baku oil business. Very likely some of their conversation was concerned with the contrast between the idealistic longing they both had for a better and more peaceful world and the destructive implements they both were engaged in manufacturing. With all his heart, Alfred

Nobel regretted the increasing military use of his inventions, which he had hoped would be used to lessen human drudgery and help promote civilization. Yet he could not help believing that advancement in every branch of science was a step ahead in human progress. And with progress, he firmly felt, would come the day when brotherhood would be a fact and civilized peace would replace barbaric war.

Alfred was right about liking Emanuel. A deep attachment sprang up between the intelligent, attractive young man and his uncle. Emanuel had been down to the Baku petroleum plant and was fascinated by it. He was sure that he wanted to make the oil industry, rather than the firearms factory, his lifework. Already he had big ideas of what he would do in Baku when he had finished his education and was put in charge of the plant there, as his father had promised.

After Alfred returned to Paris he wrote to his sister-in-law, thanking her for her kindness and contrasting his life with hers. He bewailed the fact that in spite of his wealth and position he had no cheerful memories to look back on and no comforting future to look forward to, no family, and no friends. There was no doubt that Alfred Nobel was a lonely man, but he must have been feeling exceptionally low when he wrote that letter!

8

Weapons

for

War

CROSSING THE CHILLY BALTIC SEA, Alfred thought back on the visit with Ludwig and his family. For the hundredth time he wished that he were more like this brother, who could manufacture and sell firearms without having the slightest qualms about it. Why did he, Alfred, have to be the one to inherit the gloomy temperament, the eternal worry about war and peace, right and wrong, what would help mankind's progress and what would hinder it? Scientists, he kept telling himself, were not responsible for the ways people used their inventions. Could he help it if men used his dynamite for wrong purposes? Or if armies continually struggling to improve their weapons for defense suddenly used them for aggression? Was his idea really true, he wondered, that the deadlier the weapons of war were, the less likely men would be to use them?

He stopped in Hamburg to see the other members of the German firm and to visit the factory at Krümmel. Everything was going well. Orders were coming in from all over Europe and beyond — from South Africa, South America, Canada, Australia, and Asia. Orders from distant places were being relayed to other factories, nearer to the places where they were to go.

Paul Barbe had done a good job of organization in the three years he had spent in Hamburg. He had won over the independent German competitors, as the Hamburg partners, on the spot, could not do. Alfred Nobel had never been able to secure a German patent which would shut out other German manufacturers of explosives. Now Barbe persuaded all the important explosives firms in Germany to ban together in a German Union, dividing the business and profits fairly among them all. But the Nobel British firm, the Hamburg partners told Nobel, was still undercutting prices and taking some markets which they thought rightfully belonged to them. Nobel promised to try to work this out from Paris. And he did, arranging a five-year plan of price agreement between the British and German firms and defining areas more closely.

In Paris, Nobel found a letter from Stockholm which pleased him very much. He had been elected to membership in the Royal Swedish Academy of Science. This was the finest recognition he had yet received. It put his achievements on a high scientific level and made him feel that he was really doing a worthy part in the world's work. Most honors left him cold. Once he wrote, "My decorations have no explosive basis. For my Swedish North Star I am indebted to my cook whose art appealed to an extremely aristocratic stomach. My French order I received because of my close acquaintance with a member of the cabinet; the Brazilian Order of the Rose, because I happened to be introduced to the emperor; and, finally, as far as the famous Order of Bolivar is concerned, I received that because Max Philipp [director of the German Dynamite Company] had seen *Niniche* and wanted to demonstrate how true to life was the way decorations were handed out in the play." But of membership in the Royal Swedish Academy of

Science, he wrote, "This distinction I value more than any of the others."

Nobel was eager to get out to the Sévran laboratory to start work on a dozen experiments which were buzzing about in his head. His assistant had kept busy during his absence and there were many things for them to check together. But first he must attend to the business matters which had piled high on his desk. There were also decisions waiting to be made at the Paris office. So once again Alfred Nobel curbed his impatience and delayed his scientific work while he attended to business. He had a keen sense of the value of his inventions and a sort of possessive desire to protect them from unfair exploitation. But with him, business was not an end in itself, and always he preferred a laboratory to an office.

The Scientific Advisory Board Nobel and Barbe had so hopefully set up in Paris was not doing all they had expected. Alarik Liedbeck, who headed it, was doing a fine job as a consulting engineer, giving the factories valuable technical advice, but he did not attempt to interfere in business matters. In one way there was no need. The twelve thousand employees in the various factories were satisfied. They were generously paid and fairly treated; there had never been a strike among them. But Barbe thought that the firms in the different countries were carrying on their activities too independently of one another. He believed that they should be organized in some way into a sort of "all for one, one for all" union. This would end the overlapping and competition and price wars. Investors with an interest in any one firm would profit by the gains of all the others and would help underwrite any of their possible losses. In a world-wide union Paul Barbe saw a chance of increasing his wealth and position; Alfred Nobel glimpsed the opportunity of spending more time in his precious laboratory.

As a first step, Nobel detached himself from several of the explosives companies. He sold all his shares in the American companies on both the east and the west coasts. He was not sorry to do this. He had unpleasant memories of the United States, where unscrupulous men had tried to cheat him of his rightful patent protection and profits and where, because of the nitroglycerin scare, he had been an unwelcome guest.

It took months of conferences with skillful lawyers

and scores of letters to and from the companies involved to work out a plan. It also took personal trips to the different company headquarters. Nobel traveled to England, Germany, Switzerland, and Austria. While in Vienna, he tried to see the Baroness Bertha Kinsky von Suttner — his *almost* secretary. She and her husband had recently returned from nearly ten years in the Caucasus and were happily reunited with the von Suttner family. But the von Suttners were in their country place, and though he had been warmly invited there and it was not far from Vienna, Nobel did not take the time to go.

The plan he and Paul Barbe were working on so hard was the establishing of a trust company. This was a familiar setup in American financial circles but not in Europe. The Scottish factory — the largest of the explosives plants — and the British firm — the strongest of the companies — made objections. Nobel had to use all his influence to convince them of the advantages of the trust company. At last they agreed, and in the summer of 1886, the first trust company outside America was announced in London. The Nobel Dynamite Trust Company, Ltd., was a big thing in financial circles; the capital behind it mounted into millions of dollars. Stockholders in the individual firms exchanged their shares for shares in the new, over-all company. An international board of directors was elected, with Alfred Nobel the honorary chairman and with headquarters in London.

Not all the explosives companies merged into this first trust company. The French company and other companies in southern Europe and South Africa formed a separate company called La Société Centrale de la Dynamite, with its headquarters in Paris. The Swedish and Russian firms remained independent of both trust companies.

It was a period of unrest everywhere. Modern ways of industry were changing people's lives too fast, and these rapid social changes were causing labor troubles and political violence. In this violence, dynamite played a nasty part. In the United States, dynamite bombs had been used at a mass meeting of laborers in Haymarket Square, Chicago, killing hundreds.

Once again Nobel spent weary hours pondering this problem. He knew that he was not responsible for the dynamite bombs being thrown. His business was conducted legally and openly. The explosives were sold to anyone with money to buy, like any other merchandise. There was no way an inventor could control the ways in which his product was used — or misused. And yet, as the destructive uses of dynamite increased, in a growingly restless world, its idealistic inventor shrank from what his inventions might mean. He wanted to help build a better world and a peaceful one. In his mind peace was not a separate goal but a part of the whole pattern of progress, and any contribution to science was a step ahead.

In every nation attention was being paid to the improvement of weapons. All around him, Nobel saw inventors busy devising new types of guns and cannon — putting their knowledge and skill into creating bigger and better weapons of war. With the reorganization of his companies accomplished, he was at last free to go back to his laboratory. He was still fascinated with high explosives and wanted to go on in that field. Yet he knew that almost anything he would do in it would be used for military purposes.

Again he asked himself, Would not the chances of war be cut down by deadlier weapons? Surely with war made more destructive and horrible "the whole world would revolt against the repetition of the ghastly crime and would with a unanimous acquiescence refer all disputes to a tribunal of peace." Yet in his heart Nobel must have doubted this hope which he expressed, or the problem would not have worried him so much.

Casting his doubts aside, Alfred Nobel now joined the army of chemists and physicists and engineers working on military projects. Not that he worked with them — he was always an independent, solitary inventor. Every day he went to his Sévran laboratory, where he bent over test tubes and retorts, disregarding, as always, the danger involved in working with explosive substances. And, as always, enduring the severe headaches brought on by contact with nitroglycerin. He seemed driven by an inner compulsion to get the utmost chemical returns possible from the high-explosive substances he knew so well.

A pleasant interlude in Nobel's strenuous life was the visit of the von Suttners to Paris. During the ten years they had spent in the Caucasus, both of them had become authors of some note. Artur had done journalistic pieces on interesting places, people, and events in that wild mountainous region; Bertha had written novels, which had been well received and translated into several European languages. This authorship gave the von Suttners entree into French literary circles and various authors' homes and literary *salons*. In addition, since this was Artur's first trip to Paris, they wanted to see the sights — go to the museums and theaters, saunter along the boulevards, drive in the parks, make excursions to Versailles, Saint-Cloud, and other nearby places of interest. But foremost in Bertha's mind was renewing acquaintance with Alfred Nobel.

She wrote him a note from their hotel, and by return post came a letter warmly welcoming them to Paris and setting a time when he would come to welcome them in person. "I found him unchanged," she wrote later, "except that he had grown somewhat gray, but he was more deeply than ever immersed in his labors and inventions." Nobel invited the von Suttners to his home for dinner a few nights later. There he entertained them in his usual formal, yet pleasant, fashion. Bertha was eager for her husband to see the house where she had so nearly lived, so their host took them all over it. When Artur showed interest in the chemical equipment in the laboratory and in the experiments which were under way there, the inventor took pleasure in explaining them to him in some detail.

Despite Artur von Suttner's interest in his home laboratory, Alfred Nobel did not invite him and his wife out to the larger laboratory at Sévran. It was there that Nobel was working on improving firearms, devising methods of noiseless shooting, and contriving an expanding lining to save the wear and tear on cannon bore. Some of these improvements were necessary before the more powerful explosive he had in mind could be used. To his eager, inventive mind these artillery matters were fascinating as problems; solving them brought him mental satisfaction.

The list of Nobel's English patents in the two years from 1886 to 1888 gives a glimpse into what he was doing. One patent application was headed "Improvement in explosives and their use, especially in shells and torpedoes"; it was described as being concerned with "a special fuse arrangement, devised to prevent the premature firing of the main charge by the powder thread in the time-fuse." Another patent application, headed "The regulation of pressure in guns," was described this way: "The invention consists of a piston valve with a spring contrivance, the object of which is to allow the gases to escape from the explosion chamber of the gun if the pressure should reach a strength dangerous to the structure of the gun. The contrivance closes automatically as soon as the pressure has fallen to an amount consistent with the safety of the gun, so that the escape of gas need not prejudice the speed of the projectile." Other patents had to do with the bore of a gun and with "neutralizing the recoil in firearms."

The same patent list shows that at the same time Nobel was working on firearms, he was also improving explosives for engineering purposes: "Improved detonators," "Safety explosive" ("principally designed for use in mines containing coal-dust or other explosive mine gases"), "Improvement in the manufacture of fuses."

Beyond all these inventions, Alfred Nobel was interested in the invention of a smokeless powder. This would involve combining in some way the two most powerful explosive substances — nitroglycerin and nitrocellulose. The problem attracted him theoretically, as an inventive chemist and a scientist, though he knew that a smokeless powder would be used chiefly for military purposes. He was not the only one working on this invention. German chemists were at work on it; so were chemists in Sweden and in England and in France. The French Government, which at least officially still retained its monopoly on all explosives, had scientists working in great secrecy. Their laboratory, maintained by the government, was by chance in the same little village outside Paris as Nobel's — Sévran.

It was typical of Alfred Nobel that he did not follow the same line of experimentation as the others, but struck out along an entirely new line, suggested by his study of cellulose. He still held to the two powerful explosives he knew so well — nitroglycerin and nitrocellulose — but he tried adding to them different substances and in different proportions. After many disappointments, he discovered that adding a ten-percent solution of camphor to equal parts of nitroglycerin and nitrocellulose produced a remarkable result.

It was a powder which would not explode but would burn, and only on the surface, in a precise way that could be worked out in advance. And the rate at which this powder burned was exactly related to the pressure put on it. Even such an experienced inventor as Nobel was startled by this chemical discovery. He called the product "ballistite" and took out patents on it in 1887 and 1888.

Ballistite made almost as great a stir as Nobel's earlier dynamite and blasting-gelatin inventions had done. At first even explosives experts could not believe the inventor's claims for the new product. It seemed impossible that an explosive could be pressed between warm rollers and "rolled out into thin sheets, which are cut with a knife or scissors into the desired shape and size."

Nobel's ballistite created a sensation in military circles. Army men realized at once that this invention would make great changes in the use of firearms and in army tactics. The Italian Government quickly decided to use the "Nobel powder." It contracted with the Nobel company in Italy to deliver such a large quantity that an addition had to be built onto the Italian factory for the sole purpose of making ballistite for the Italian Government. At first the government paid a royalty on what it bought; then it paid the Nobel company a large sum for the right to manufacture ballistite itself.

The British Government, according to its custom, began a slow and extensive investigation of this new invention. One of the members of the committee appointed to look into the values and uses of ballistite was Professor Frederick Abel. Twenty years before, when dynamite was new, he had been on the committee appointed to investigate it. He had strongly opposed importing dynamite into England. Nobel had had to prove to Abel's satisfaction that dynamite was less dangerous than guncotton before England accepted it. After dynamite had won out in England, a sort of professional friendship had sprung up between Abel and Nobel. They exchanged letters on technical subjects and sometimes met in Paris or London. Now Professor Abel asked Nobel's help in informing the committee on the principles behind the new invention and any new methods he developed for its manufacture. Nobel cooperated willingly, foreseeing a market for ballistite with the British Government. He never dreamed that Abel and a scientist friend were using his information to guide them in working out a similar smokeless powder, which they hoped would be adopted by the British Government.

The French Government did not like the news of Nobel's new discovery, or the idea of Italy's buying it. This was not only a matter of pride or even the fear of another country's getting a powerful weapon of war. It was also the thought of the financial loss to France with Nobel's invention winning out over the smokeless powder which was being developed in their own plant at Sévran. Some of the officials of the government explosives monopoly began to circulate the ugly rumor that the Swedish inventor might have spied on the French chemists. The newspapers saw a sensational story in this absolutely unfounded rumor and played it up for all it was worth. Nobel tried to disregard the unpleasant publicity by keeping to himself and continuing his work without comment.

For he was a perfectionist. He did not rest content with his ballistite invention as it was first patented and manufactured, but went on trying to improve it.

Within a year he had taken out another patent on a simpler method of manufacture which did away entirely with solvents.

One hesitates to think of the physical risks involved in making the experiments which led to this discovery. One thing is sure — for many people testified to this over the inventor's lifetime — Alfred Nobel always made the most dangerous tests himself before he would direct anyone else to make them.

The attitude of the French Government and the French press grew more and more hostile toward Alfred Nobel. And this came at a very bad time for him, for several reasons.

Within two years' time he lost both his brother Ludwig and his mother. Ludwig had refused to slow down his fast pace, his frequent traveling from northern to southern Russia, his energetic work both in St. Petersburg and at Baku. In 1887, he had to give in to the doctor's orders. Putting Emanuel in charge of the Nobel Brothers' Naphtha Company, and the younger Carl at the head of the St. Petersburg machinery plant, he went to southern France to try to recover his health. But it was too late. His illness was too far advanced, and he died on the French Riviera the following spring.

By some mischance, the French newspapers confused names. Instead of printing an obituary of Ludwig Nobel the oil tycoon, they printed one of Alfred Nobel the dynamite king. It was rather upsetting to Alfred to read his own death notices. And, though not particularly surprising, it was not very pleasant to see how much the French press seemed to dislike him.

When, the next year, his mother died in Stockholm at the good old age of eighty-six, Alfred felt lonely indeed. "She loved me as people do not love nowadays," he wrote Bertha von Suttner in a letter written on his way back to Paris after the funeral. Alfred had remained close to his mother always, and he missed her greatly. His many gifts had made her a rich woman; his letters and visits, a happy one. She had called him her "dear, good boy" and her "beloved Alfred," and she had passed on many of his gifts to others who needed them more than she did. After her death, Alfred continued her good works by giving his third of her estate to her friends and to various charitable institutions in which she was interested, including a children's hospital.

Alfred Nobel had heard rumors of Paul Barbe's political involvements, and they did not make pleasant listening. He once declared that his partner had an "elastic conscience." But he had figured that Barbe's political life was his own affair and he kept strictly out of it. He knew that Barbe was an ambitious man and that he was willing to use his wealth and his influence in somewhat questionable ways in order to gain a high place in the French Government.

Barbe was elected a deputy in the French legislature; then he was made minister of agriculture. While he was a deputy, he was on a committee appointed to investigate a "lottery loan" to the Panama Canal Company — the company which had been organized to finance the construction of the Panama Canal. Because of mismanagement and engineering difficulties, the company needed more money. To get buyers for a new bond issue, cash prizes were offered to holders of lucky-numbered bonds. There was a question whether this was legal, and it was said that many politicians were bribed to vote for the lottery loan idea. In spite of this, the bill lost. Barbe voted against it, partly, he admitted, because the dynamite being used in the

Panama Canal construction was bought in the United States instead of from companies in which he had an interest. Two years later, the matter came up again. By then, by strange coincidence, the Panama Canal Company was buying its dynamite from La Société Centrale de la Dynamite, and Barbe helped pass the Lottery Loan Authorization bill.

Alfred Nobel did not realize that the feeling which the French people were beginning to express against their unscrupulous politicians would carry over to him. Yet later it was clear that Barbe's actions influenced the attitude of the French newspapers in their unfair attack on Nobel after the ballistite sale to Italy. Something else happened. In Barbe's struggle for power he spoke out sharply against one of his political enemies. Soon afterward this man became premier of France, and he saw in Barbe's connection with the Nobel explosives an indirect way of taking revenge on Barbe.

One morning early in the spring of 1890, police arrived at Alfred Nobel's Sévran laboratory. They had orders to search the place, though they did not know exactly what it was they were supposed to find.

They looked about in a clumsy way and took a small amount of the smokeless powder. Then, in the name of the government, they turned out the owner and his assistant and padlocked the door. They also forbade him the use of the little shooting range near the laboratory, where he had installed some small cannon to test out his artillery inventions. And this in spite of Nobel's having paid the government well for permission to use this place, which was part of an old, abandoned fort. In addition, the government forbade the Nobel French dynamite factory from manufacturing any ballistite.

Nobel wrote his favorite nephew, Emanuel, about it. "The government, by virtue of its monopoly," he wrote, "has prohibited me from making even the smallest amount of explosive, or possessing any kind of weapon for my shooting tests." He went on to say that the penalty for disobedience would be imprisonment, and he hesitated at that because he was afraid it might be hard on his already poor digestion! "Not to be allowed to work at Sévran has pretty well upset my applecart," he wrote. "I was in the middle of some very interesting problems which will have to be put aside." But there was nothing he could do against the French Government.

Alfred Nobel started again to work in the laboratory in his home. Restless and at loose ends, he gave more thought to his poor health than he had done for many years. Was Ludwig's early death, he wondered, a warning of what would happen to him? He had told one of the lecturers at the medical institute in Stockholm that he would be interested in meeting a young physiologist who might come to Paris to work with him on a series of medical investigations. Now, in the fall of 1890, when the trouble with the French Government was at its height, Herre Johannsson responded. Nobel was glad to have a new line of interest to occupy his mind and time.

He told the young man that he felt more should be done to determine the body's own ways of curing diseases. A scientist with physiological rather than medical training might approach the subject with more freedom, he thought. He would like Herre Johannsson to undertake a number of different kinds of experimental medical research. And so the young man settled down in the big house, staying for five months.

He carried on various tests and experiments, among them a series of experiments in blood transfusion. Nobel was interested, though preoccupied with the trouble with the government. He told Johannsson that he often wished his activities along other lines would leave him more time to devote himself to medical research. And he said that he had in mind founding a center for experimental medical research. His own successful use of experimental methods made him think the same technique could be used in the medical field.

But life without the kind of laboratory he needed soon grew intolerable to such an inveterate inventor. So did the strained relations with the government under which he lived. If France did not want him, other countries did. His German friends urged him to come back to Hamburg. And so he sent Johannsson back to Sweden, outlined various experiments and activities for Fehrenbach, and went to Hamburg. He was made very welcome there; he had a laboratory at his disposal in the Krümmel plant and the best suite in the finest Hamburg hotel. But Germany did not appeal to him as a permanent home.

Then came news of the sudden death of Paul Barbe in Paris. This shocked Nobel, as did the news of some of the financial speculations in which, it seemed, his French partner had involved the French dynamite company without his knowledge. For a few hours Nobel wondered if his great fortune might all have oozed away while he had kept himself buried in his laboratory. Might he have to stay on in Hamburg, employed by the firm he had founded? His common sense told him better, and he hurried back to Paris.

At the headquarters of La Société Centrale de la Dynamite, Nobel went to work in earnest. He went over the books and discovered that, by putting in a considerable amount himself, the company could weather the storm and meet the losses that Paul Barbe had brought upon it. He threw out of the organization the men Barbe had brought in and found a capable Frenchman of good reputation to put in charge, in Barbe's place. He set up a closer association with the British dynamite company so that it would have some voice in the management of the Société Centrale. Within a few weeks he completely cleared up the unsavory mess left by Paul Barbe. Then — but not till then — he resigned from the presidency of the Société Centrale and from the boards of its various member firms.

Alfred Nobel had had enough of France. He was ready to live somewhere else. Not Germany, nor England, nor Sweden — yet. He thought with warmth of the friendly Italians, of his pleasant relations with their government, of the flourishing Italian explosives firm which bore his name, and of the balmy air and beautiful scenery of sunny Italy. That same year he closed the Paris house, took what he was allowed to take from the Sévran laboratory, and left for Italy.

He invited his assistant to come with him, but Georg Fehrenbach, understandably enough, preferred to remain in his native land. Not much is known of this young French chemist who came to be the inventor's laboratory assistant when he first moved to Paris and who stayed with him the entire eighteen years of his Paris residence. One of the assistant's duties was to keep the laboratory journal, an invaluable record of the many experiments made. Most of them led to nothing, it seemed, yet they contributed to the knowledge which made possible the others, the highly successful ones. Georg Fehrenbach must have felt tremendous pride in these successful accomplishments and a great respect and fondness for his talented employer.

In the little town of San Remo, among the palms and orange trees of the Italian Riviera, Alfred Nobel bought a villa. And there, in 1891, he established his residence.

9

Which
Way
to Peace?

THE SOFT AIR and natural loveliness of the Italian Riviera helped raise Alfred Nobel's spirits. From Paris he had written a Stockholm friend, "I am worn out." Here in San Remo he found it relaxing to walk beside the blue sea and to sleep with the soothing sound of its shore-lapping waves in his ears. The big villa was comfortable. He felt at home in it and called it Mio Nido — My Nest. The grounds which surrounded the house were lovely with gardens and trees — mimosa and orange and lemon trees, pines and palms. Everywhere to the south were the long seaward vistas, and to the north, the distant mountain views.

Mio Nido did not long remain so lazily peaceful.

With the help of his faithful old butler Auguste, the house was refurnished to its new owner's liking and the other servants brought down from the Paris house to run it. Then Nobel turned his attention to setting up his laboratory. This was not so simple. Most of the things he needed — mechanical equipment, laboratory apparatus, chemicals — he could not buy in San Remo or, in fact, in all Italy; he had to send to Hamburg for them.

While he waited for these essentials and for the equipment from his Paris laboratory, Nobel had a long, low building put up to his specifications in a little grove of young citrus trees near the sea. There were plenty of windows to bring in the southern light, as well as shades to shut it out when it was too strong. Inside were three rooms. One was for the heavy machines — electrical generators and the most modern mechanical equipment available. Another was the laboratory proper, with counters and tables, heating and testing apparatus, running water, rollers, weighing and pressure machines, cases of chemicals. The third room held various small instruments and rows of bookcases filled with scientific books.

To take the place of the old shooting range at Sévran, Nobel had a long steel pier built out into the Mediterranean. From here he would be able to test his artillery-improvement inventions, shooting guns and cannon any distance at all and measuring their speeds on a precision instrument called a chronograph.

But if Nobel thought he would be quite without troubles in this peaceful spot, he was mistaken. When the owner of the villa next to his saw the long, low building going up and the ugly steel pier jutting out into the sea, and heard what they were to be used for, he was horrified. For some time he had wanted to sell his place; now he was afraid that with a laboratory next door where explosives were tested and a pier from which cannon might go booming out over the sea at any hour, no one would want to buy his house — at his price. And so he raised a hue and cry about the danger of the inventor's activities and their nuisance to the neighborhood. He even threatened to go into court about it.

Alfred Nobel wanted no more trouble with courts. Without a word to the irate neighbor, he quietly arranged to buy his house. He did not quibble about the price. As soon as the place was vacated, he had the hedge that separated the two estates torn down and he instructed his gardeners to take care of the additional grounds. The house remained empty for several years before he finally had it fixed up as a guest-house, fit for a king.

Now at last the inventor was free to work without any outside interference. He wrote many letters trying to locate just the right laboratory assistant to take the place of Georg Fehrenbach, who had stayed behind in Paris. At last he engaged a young Englishman by the name of Beckett.

As soon as everything was in readiness and Mr. Beckett was on hand, work began. To Nobel's delight, the climate was so mild that he could continue with his outdoor experiments throughout the winter months. He went on with the artillery improvements he had been working on in Paris, carefully explaining to Mr. Beckett that it was the theoretical, scientific challenge of these problems which fascinated him. Nor did he seem to care too much when some of the weapons he worked out had no real practical value.

Among these artillery inventions were several connected with rockets and the means of firing them. During these first years in Italy Alfred Nobel applied for a number of patents along this line. One was described as a "Method for causing rockets and other projectiles to rotate." There was also a rocket projectile which the inventor thought could be used to rescue survivors on a shipwrecked vessel. He succeeded in sending it a distance of almost three miles but never got the aim quite accurate enough to make it of practical use.

Alfred Nobel was, without doubt, fascinated by the challenge of solving artillery and rocket problems. Yet he was even more interested in the possibilities he saw in nitrocellulose. As he found more ways to dissolve it, he discovered that many of the solvents could be used to manufacture varnishes and dyes. To his amazement he found that, going a step beyond this, he was uncovering ways of making artificial rubber, leather, and silk. Here was a whole new field for exploration! Five of his English patents, taken out in 1893 and 1894, were concerned with these altogether new ideas.

Two other patents were labeled "Improvements in

phonographs and telephones," and "Improvements in electric batteries." There was nothing single-tracked about Alfred Nobel's inventive genius! He was not always a good judge of the practical use of his ideas, but many inventions which others scoffed at were, like his father's plywood, merely ahead of the times. This greater interest in industrial inventions may have been partly the result of his changing ideas toward war and peace — a change brought about, at least in part, by the Baroness Bertha von Suttner.

The winter Bertha and Artur von Suttner were in Paris they heard of an English organization called the International Peace and Arbitration Association. Its purpose was to promote the idea of an international court to settle disputes between nations, in place of war. Both the Suttners became deeply interested in this peace movement, but especially Bertha. She read every word of its appeal for membership, from its beginning: "Lately a member of the English ministry declared that England's greatest interest is peace. Could not the same thing be said of every civilized country?" to its last sentence, which suggested the forming of "a great league, with branches in all European cities."

On her return to Austria, Bertha von Suttner decided to help the cause of peace by making it the theme of her next novel. She created as her heroine a young woman to whom war brought romance, suffering, and tragedy. She was deeply moved as she wrote the story, which was really a powerful appeal in fictional form, for peace. She entitled it *Die Waffen Nieder*, which the English translated variously as *No More War!*, *Away with Weapons!*, and *Lay Down Arms!*

Because everything she had written had been accepted for publication at once, Bertha was surprised and distressed to have such a hard time getting *Die Waffen Nieder* into print. No magazine would take it for fear of offending some government official. Even her book publisher begged her to change the title and to let someone go over the story to take out any parts which might give offense. But Bertha felt too strongly about it. She would not change a word. Fearfully the publisher brought out the book — and overnight it became a huge success. It was enthusiastically received in Austria and Germany, was translated into several languages and read all over Europe. The reason, its author was sure, was that the idea of peace was "cherished in wide circles — even in military circles."

Among the hundreds of letters she received about her book was one from Alfred Nobel. He complimented her on her "masterpiece" and praised her for "so valiantly making war on war." Up to this time the correspondence between the two had been only occasional and purely social. Now it became a frequent exchange of news and views on the subject which interested them both so deeply.

Writing the book, and the relationships which grew out of it, swept Bertha von Suttner heart-first into the growing peace movement. She organized the Austrian Peace Society, and it immediately made her its delegate to the International Peace Congress to be held in Rome. There she delivered a speech — the first woman at the congress to do so — and her intense feeling made a deep impression on the audience. Back in Vienna she became editor of a Berlin-published magazine devoted to peace and called by the title of her book. The promotion of peace became the most important thing in the world to her (aside from the still-flourishing romance with Artur) and she gave to it practically all her time and energy. She wrote and spoke continually, urging people everywhere to work for peace.

When the cause needed money, the baroness cared enough, proud noblewoman though she was, to write to sympathetic friends for funds. She wrote to Alfred Nobel, and he responded with a check, but also with the warning that what the peace movement needed more than money was a definite program, a practical plan. And he proceeded to outline this plan.

Alfred Nobel's plan for peace was not written off the top of his head. He had been thinking seriously about the problems of peace and war far longer than Bertha von Suttner. All his life he had considered war one of the greatest evils of human life. He had tried to believe that if war became terrible enough, no nation would dare begin one. And so, as he improved the weapons of war and made them more destructive, he told himself that he was really working toward peace. This was perhaps why, as one of his closest associates states, "when he turned to more military inventions (about 1887) he also turned more strongly toward pacifism."

In Paris, a few months before he left to live in San Remo, Nobel told a friend that he had decided explosives alone would not keep men from waging war. They were too limited in space and effectiveness. But wars would stop instantly, he said, if war meant death for the general as well as for the soldier, or if war "hovered impartially over every man, woman, and child." And he concluded, "The only thing that will ever prevent nations from beginning war is terror."

Now, only a year or two later, he must have had doubts about this terror theory. His plan for peace, set forth in this letter to Bertha von Suttner, written in late 1891, was based on a quite different idea. It would not demand disarmament or the immediate establishment of a court of arbitration, as the peace organizations were intent on doing, but would be "content to begin more modestly" by presenting to European governments a proposal, backed by noted statesmen, to allow a year for arbitration of disputes with other nations before going to war.

"Would it be too much to ask," he went on, "that for one year the European governments should undertake to refer to a court formed for this purpose any differences arising between them; or if they should refuse to take this step, to postpone any act of hostility until the expiration of the period stipulated? This would seem to be little, but it is just by being content with little that one arrives at great results. A year is a short time in the life of a nation. . . . And at the expiration of that period all the nations would quickly renew their peace compact for another year. Thus, without shock and almost without realizing the fact, a long period of peace would be secured."

But this little-by-little plan of Alfred Nobel was too slow for Bertha von Suttner's ardent heart. Peace, she thought, was just around the corner. It was not too much to expect disarmament, she wrote him, and soon. And she urged him to come to the Peace Congress at Bern the next year. There he would learn first-hand of the progress and plans of the peace movement. To this invitation Alfred Nobel did not say yes and he did not say no.

Bertha von Suttner and her husband were key

figures at the fourth World's Peace Congress in Bern, Switzerland, in August, 1892. One afternoon when some of them were relaxing on the hotel veranda, an attendant brought to the baroness the card of a gentleman who was waiting in the parlors to see her. It was Alfred Nobel.

"You called me," he said. "Here I am. But incognito, so to speak. I do not want to take part in the congress or make any acquaintances; only to hear something specific about the matter. Tell me what has been done so far."

They talked for a long time. Before Nobel left that evening he made Bertha and Artur promise to pay him a visit at Zurich, where he was staying for a time, as soon as the congress was over.

Alfred Nobel met the Suttners at the Zurich railroad station. He took them to the hotel, where he had reserved a luxurious suite of rooms for them. At dinner, in a dining room with breath-taking views of snowy mountaintops reflected in the quiet lake, he asked his guests to tell him all about the congress. And he gave them his name for membership in the Austrian Peace Society and a check for its work. The baroness accepted it graciously, though she said she feared it came "more from amiability than from conviction."

Her host smiled. He said he had no doubts about the justice of the cause, but he admitted that he did have doubts about the way the peace organizations were trying to realize it.

"If you knew the work was being well taken hold of, would you take a hand and help?" Bertha asked eagerly.

"Yes," he answered, "I would. Inform me; convince me; and I will do something great for the movement."

Bertha von Suttner beamed. She could hardly meet that challenge over dessert, she said, but in the next few days she would try not only to convince him but to make him enthusiastic.

The weary inventor sighed. "Good!" he said. "I would like nothing better than to feel enthusiasm for something."

For several days the two of them talked for hours each day, while Artur sat beside them, quietly listening. Bertha's ideas were quick, fervent, and inclined a little toward the sentimental. Alfred Nobel's suggestions were thoughtful, cautious, and practical.

Once again he brought out the argument which had reassured him when he saw large government orders for his dynamite or when he worked on making a rifle more effective. "The more terrible the means of destruction, the more nations will wish to escape the responsibility of declaring war. Perhaps my dynamite factories will put an end to war sooner than your congresses. On the day when two army corps are able to annihilate each other in a second, probably all civilized nations will recoil from war in horror and disband their troops."

Both Bertha and Artur shook their heads vigorously at this theory. While Bertha was thinking up a good answer to it, Nobel went on:

"My countryman, John Ericsson, held much the same idea when he invented destroyers. Ericsson's principal object was to make maritime war impossible and to force all nations to recognize the neutrality of the sea. I have read that he said, 'The art of war is in its infancy. Brought to perfection, it will oblige men to live in peace.' He called this a 'sublime object' and said that it was the cherished dream of his life."

They were all silent as they thought about this

ideal and the people everywhere who shared it. Then Nobel said aloud, "I could truthfully make that statement with my countryman, though I confess I do not have the faith he had that the goal will be reached before the end of this century. I believe it will come more slowly. And I sincerely believe that gradual steps toward arbitration are the best way to achieve it."

Bertha von Suttner did not try to answer. This time it was she who was impressed but not convinced.

Not all the time at Zurich was spent in serious conversation. The three of them visited interesting places in the city; they made excursions to nearby scenic spots; they took rides on the lovely lake. Nobel had on it a motorboat which was something of a curiosity. It was made entirely of aluminum except for a single copper steam pipe. The inventor had taken a great interest in aluminum and had sensed the possibilities of using this light, malleable metal to replace some of the more commonly used heavier metals. In order to have a better chance to experiment with it, he had bought an interest in a Swiss aluminum works near Zurich. This was the business which had brought him to Switzerland, and the motorboat was one result of his experiments. It had great speed and moved smoothly over the water, without any rocking from side to side.

"We sat leaning back in comfortable deck chairs covered with soft plaids," wrote Bertha as she recalled the scene years later. "We let the magic panorama of the lake shores pass before our eyes and talked about a thousand things between heaven and earth."

They even dreamed of writing a book together — a book in which they would rail against all the things that keep the world living "stupidly and wretchedly" instead of in a golden era of knowledge and peace. It was technical discoveries which would bring about this golden age, Alfred Nobel firmly believed. "Every new discovery modifies the human brain," he stated, "and makes the new generation capable of receiving new ideas." The progress of science, he thought, would result in general prosperity, and this, he felt, would do away with most of the evils inherited from the past.

The happy vacation days at Lake Zurich passed all too swiftly. The Suttners bade a reluctant good-by to their host, with Bertha promising to keep him informed about the progress of the peace movement.

They headed back to Vienna, and he finished his work in Switzerland and went on to Paris.

Alfred Nobel now felt definitely committed to do something for the peace movement. But he had seen the peace organizations in their congress and he did not have much faith in accomplishing anything practical through them. He was afraid that any common-sense approach would be delayed or spoiled by the many "windbag" members. He preferred to work by himself, and in Zurich he had thought of a way to do this.

Months before, some of Nobel's Swedish friends in Paris — among them the Swedish-Norwegian minister to France — had spoken to him about a Turkish diplomat named Aristarchi Bey, who had been the Turkish ambassador to the United States and was now retired and living insecurely in Paris. Could Nobel find a place for him in one of his business firms? Nobel had promised to try, but nothing suitable had turned up. Now he wondered if this might not be the very man to carry forward his peace plan. As a professional diplomat Aristarchi Bey would know the proper men to approach in the various governments and how to interest them in the idea of international arbitration.

Alfred Nobel was not a man to hang back when he determined on a course of action. He wired Aristarchi Bey from Zurich to make sure he was still available. Then he wrote the man a long letter, outlining his ideas and saying that it would please him to carry the work of the Peace Congress forward even a step, no matter what the expense.

Soon after arriving in Paris, Nobel had a conference with Aristarchi Bey. He was favorably impressed with the man and with his fitness for this particular task. They agreed that for a year Aristarchi Bey should work on influencing the press and important men in governmental positions toward peace. Nobel offered him a liberal salary and freedom to discontinue the arrangement at any time he wished to make some other connection. Of all this, Alfred Nobel did not write the baroness a word.

Aristarchi Bey entered into the agreement with enthusiasm. But he argued against one point of the plan so logically that he changed Nobel's thinking on it. No nation, he pointed out, would be willing to sacrifice its advantage of a quick surprise attack on an enemy by

delaying a year for arbitration which might end unsuccessfully.

"I am beginning to believe," Alfred Nobel wrote a
Belgian pacifist, "that the only true solution would be
a convention under which all the governments would
bind themselves to defend collectively any country
that was attacked." A little later he wrote a letter to
Bertha von Suttner, setting forth this same revolutionary idea which, almost thirty years later, became a
cornerstone of the League of Nations. "Peace, guaran-
teed by the power of collective armies," he wrote,
"would soon relieve the tension; and from year to
year we would see the strength of standing armies in
the various countries being reduced cautiously but
surely."

The baroness did not agree with Nobel's new line
of thought. She still believed in arbitration and disarmament, and she sent him some of the organization's
literature on the subject to prove her points. But he
stuck to his new-found belief that the best way to prevent war was by a joint military action against any
country that broke the peace.

In January that same winter, Alfred Nobel had another brainstorm. In a letter to Bertha von Suttner he suggested an entirely new idea. "I should like," he wrote, "to allot part of my fortune to the founding of a prize to be awarded every five years — say six times, for if we have failed in thirty years to reform the present system we shall inevitably fall back into barbarism. This prize would be awarded to the man or woman who had done the most to advance the idea of general peace in Europe. I am not speaking of disarmament, which can be achieved only by slow degrees. I am not even speaking of compulsory arbitration among nations. What I have in mind is that we should be able to reach rather soon the point where all nations would bind themselves to take action against the first aggressor. Wars will then be impossible, and even the most quarrelsome state would be forced to appeal to a court or else remain quiet."

Bertha, although she did not agree with Nobel's methods, was glad to get the letter. At least he was still sincerely and actively interested in the cause of peace. In time, she thought, he would see things her way.

The Aristarchi Bey arrangement did not turn out

well. The man could not seem to catch Nobel's point of view or carry through the projects he had in mind. Aristarchi Bey had fewer connections in governmental circles than Nobel had thought, and he did not succeed in getting any articles on peace published in leading European newspapers, as Nobel had hoped he might do. When Aristarchi Bey suggested that they start a periodical devoted to peace, Alfred Nobel reminded him that Baroness von Suttner was the editor of just such a magazine and there was no need for another. Magazines like this, Nobel pointed out, were read by those who already believed in peace, not by people who needed to have their interest in the cause awakened.

Nothing really constructive came from Aristarchi Bey the whole year, much to Alfred Nobel's disappointment. Yet when, toward the end of the year, Nobel told him that the contract would not be renewed, he was quite disagreeable about it. He claimed that he had turned down an offer in the sultan's diplomatic services because he had expected this connection to be permanent. When Nobel remained firm, Aristarchi Bey asked that their difference be arbitrated; then he threatened his employer with legal action.

At this, Nobel sent him a frank letter. "I have loyally carried out the year's experiment," he wrote, "but I find that you have not carried the matter forward one step. I do not know of a single article emanating from your pen that deals with this subject. Neither am I aware that you have converted to the cause sponsored by Frau von Suttner a single person of importance. . . . Considering how little occasion I have had to make use of your special gifts, I cannot see how you could imagine that such an unusual arrangement should be extended beyond the period originally agreed upon." And he could not resist ending on the sour note that it seemed as if every time he did someone a favor he had reason to regret it.

Alfred Nobel did not try to find a successor to Aristarchi Bey. In spite of his disappointment in the year's experiment, it had been a good thing for the inventor. It had made him think through his own beliefs and approaches to the whole subject of peace. It had given him an insight into the practices of diplomacy and statesmanship. Because of this thinking, his ideas on how to achieve a peaceful world had developed more than a little during the year.

For one thing, the thought of the peace prize ripened into determination, though in slightly different form. A few weeks after he wrote the letter to Bertha von Suttner suggesting the idea, Nobel made a will. In it, after leaving about a fifth of his estate to relatives and friends and another fifth to various institutions, he directed that the balance should make up a fund whose interest should be distributed annually "as a reward for the most important and original discoveries or intellectual achievements in the wide field of knowledge and progress," with particular consideration for persons who were "successful in word and deed in combating the peculiar prejudices still cherished by peoples and governments against the inauguration of a European peace tribunal."

In his thinking Alfred Nobel seemed to be coming back to the belief he had held earlier that peace was only a part, though an important part, in the whole great picture of progress. As mankind grew wiser, wars would become outmoded and lasting peace would be achieved. Every advance in science was a step toward a better and more peaceful world. Perhaps the words of Pasteur, whom he admired, rang in his ears: "It is ignorance which separates men, and science which brings them together."

10

Emphasis

on

Sweden

ALFRED NOBEL was far from being a proud man, but
he was both pleased and proud when in June, 1893,
the ancient and highly respected Swedish University
of Uppsala gave him the honorary degree of Doctor
of Philosophy. For a man who had never been to college — who, in fact, had scarcely been to school at all
— this was an unusual honor and a tribute to his accomplishments. Nobel valued it for sentimental reasons, too, since it came from the university which the
much-loved, ill-fated Emil had attended and also, two
centuries earlier, his great-great-grandfather, Petrus
Nobelius. Now on formal occasions the inventor was
addressed as Dr. Nobel and treated with the respect

due one of the leading scientists of the age. Yet he remained as retiring and considerate as he had always been. Becoming a Doctor of Philosophy had made him "almost more of a philosopher than before," he jokingly wrote to his old friend Alarik Liedbeck.

Too many of the people claiming friendship with Dr. Nobel were looking for some favor from him and he knew it. But Alarik Liedbeck was not one of them. He had been one of Nobel's closest friends since the days when he was manager of the Swedish factory. From there Liedbeck had gone to Scotland to help Alfred Nobel construct and start the Ardeer plant, then to Krümmel, and then to Paris to be the consulting engineer for all the factories. Like Nobel, Liedbeck was both a brilliant man and a modest one. Like Nobel, too, he had great physical courage, as any man in charge of a dynamite factory needed to have. Nobel often turned to Liedbeck to construct the apparatus for testing a new invention or for manufacturing it. The two men understood each other so well that they could work out intricate mechanical matters through correspondence. A few patents, Nobel insisted on applying for in both their names, and he appreciated the fact that his inventions were often made more practical by Liedbeck's skillful work.

After the deaths of his brother Ludwig and his mother, Alfred Nobel leaned more heavily on his few close friends. There never were many of these. "You refer to my 'numerous' friends," he wrote someone. "Where are they? They are stuck fast in the morass of lost illusions or in the bogs of money-making."

Alfred had never been quite so close to Robert and his family as to Ludwig and his boys, particularly Ludwig's oldest son, Emanuel. Between this nephew and his uncle there was deep understanding and real affection. Occasionally they met in Vienna, Berlin, or Paris, and they wrote each other fairly often, in spite of their busy lives. Emanuel kept his uncle informed on developments at Baku and frequently asked his advice. Emanuel was as industrious as his father and his uncle, and had carried on the work at Baku with great success. He had enlarged the plant and expanded the business. He also had done everything possible for the well-being and happiness of his employees.

In addition to the friendship of Liedbeck and Emanuel, a friendship which meant much to Alfred No-

bel in the later years of his life was that of a young man
named Ragnar Sohlman. In the fall of 1893, Sohlman
came to Nobel to be his personal assistant. He had
been recommended by Herre Smitt of Stockholm —
the same Herre Smitt who had put up the money to
form the first nitroglycerin company and who now
was head of the Swedish Nobel Dynamite Company.
Sohlman had also been recommended by Robert Nobel's second son, Ludwig, a schoolmate at the Stockholm Institute of Technology. After passing his final
examinations, young Sohlman had gone to America
to be a chemist in a dynamite factory. But times were
bad in America just then and the future did not look
bright for him. He was working in the Swedish pavil-
ion at the Chicago World's Fair when he received a
cable from home, telling him that he had been offered
the position of personal assistant to Dr. Alfred Nobel.
He accepted immediately and was instructed to go to
Paris to meet his future employer.

Nobel had retained his Paris house. A small staff of
servants kept everything in order and others went up
from San Remo whenever Nobel was to be in Paris. It
was here that Ragnar Sohlman had his appointment.

He felt a bit nervous and ill at ease as Auguste, the butler, took him to the study. At the big desk he saw a man of about sixty, with "strongly marked features, a high forehead, bushy eyebrows, and somewhat deep-set eyes whose glance was both keen and changeable."

Nobel was so cordial and natural that the young man's nervousness soon disappeared. They talked together about Sohlman's experiences in America and their mutual friends in Stockholm. Sohlman found himself telling Nobel about a trip he had taken one summer, when he was a student, on an empty Nobel oil tanker going from the Swedish shipyards across the Baltic and down the Russian inland-water route to the Caspian Sea. There, at the Baku clubhouse for the Nobel employees, he had talked with Robert Nobel and his oldest son, Hjalmar, both of whom he had met before in Stockholm.

Ragnar Sohlman's first assignment was to put the Paris library and correspondence files in order. This gave the two men a chance to become acquainted. When Nobel discovered that Sohlman was far more interested in chemistry than in matters related to the work of a personal secretary, he sent him down to San

Remo to work with Beckett in the laboratory there.

The two young men — Beckett the Englishman and Sohlman the Swede — got on well together. Sohlman was delighted to find such a completely equipped private laboratory. Beckett showed him everything, and he immediately began to help with the experiments in process. When, two or three weeks later, Alfred Nobel appeared, the three of them worked in the laboratory together. Each day Nobel would check up on the progress of the experiments and give directions for the next steps to be taken.

They were trying to perfect various new types of almost smokeless gunpowder and were also working out new kinds of fuses for blasting operations. In addition, Nobel was attempting to produce from nitrocellulose artificial substitutes for rubber and leather. Noticing Sohlman's fascination with this project, the inventor gave him the special assignment of finding and testing solvents which would combine with low-nitrated cellulose to produce elastic or solidly gelatinized substances. If they were successful, Nobel hoped to establish an important new industry.

Although the inventor was intensely interested in

this laboratory work, he was also very busy that winter with two other projects, one of them pleasant, the other unpleasant. The pleasant project was the purchase of a place in Sweden. The unpleasant project was the preparation of his defense in a case to come up in the English courts.

Nobel had been upset and distressed when he learned of the action his English friend Abel and Abel's associate Dewar had taken after checking with him on his ballistite invention three or four years before. Without a word to him they had gone ahead with independent experiments, had worked out a modification of his smokeless powder, and had patented it as their own under the name of cordite. They had given it this name because of its ribbed appearance, but the only real difference between it and Nobel's powder was that cordite used an insoluble nitrocellulose with the nitroglycerin, while in ballistite Nobel had used a soluble nitrocellulose, usually camphor. Abel and Dewar had made over their English patent rights on cordite to the British Government but had kept all foreign rights for themselves.

Nobel had not known a thing about the cordite invention until the British War Office announced its decision to use cordite in the British Army and Navy. This would, of course, have been a big market for ballistite. After Nobel had looked into the cordite-invention matter carefully, he protested, claiming that cordite was based on his ballistite, which was protected by patent. When his protests got nowhere, Nobel decided to submit the matter to the British courts in a "friendly suit."

It was a complicated case, and one which attracted much attention in the scientific world. And no wonder, for the plaintiff was the powerful Nobel Explosives Company of Glasgow; the defendant, the British Government; the complaint, infringement of Alfred Nobel's ballistite patent.

That winter in San Remo, Nobel spent many hours comparing notes and going over correspondence. From them he proved beyond doubt that he had given Abel and Dewar information which was of assistance to them in working out their formula for cordite. The more Nobel worked on the case the more the injustice of the English action and the disillusionment in his friends upset him. He lost his never-too-good appetite and had severe headaches, which he tried to disregard. He would sit at his desk with wet towels wrapped about his head, writing letters and making notes. When his nervousness and misery grew too acute to go on, he would read or try to make some progress on the play he was attempting to write. He had never wholly given up the idea of writing. He had some ability in that direction, as his well-expressed letters showed, and he enjoyed setting forth his ideas in poetic, fictional, or dramatic form. Writing took his mind off his illness or his worries.

Another favorite diversion was driving. He would call for his carriage and a pair of his thoroughbred horses and go for a drive on the hillside roads, some of them there since Roman days. He delighted in the distant vistas of mountains to the north and the broad expanse of the blue Mediterranean far below. Often he would invite one or both of his assistants to go driving with him.

The friendship with Sohlman was deepening. Nobel found it both stimulating and relaxing to be with this dependable young man who seemed fascinated by the same technical problems which attracted him. It was restful, too, to lapse into the mother tongue, Swedish, in place of English, which was the common language when he and his two assistants talked together, or French, which he spoke to his servants. And it was pleasant to talk about Sweden, the Swedish people they both knew, and the prospect of spending more time there as soon as this troublesome English lawsuit was over.

In spite of all the years away and his natural internationalism, Alfred Nobel still considered himself a Swede and Sweden his homeland. Ever since receiving the Uppsala honorary degree — and subconsciously probably earlier — his heart had been set on eventually getting back to his native country. He could live and work in Sweden during the warmer part of the year, spend the winter in sunny San Remo, and stop over in Paris for a month or two on the way there and back. Having made up his mind to the move, he began to look for a place in Sweden where he could have a home, a laboratory, and a factory. In this way he could carry on experiments on a larger scale than was possible at San Remo; he might also put some of the successful inventions into production.

He discarded the first place offered him — an ancient brassworks with a magnificent castle nearby — because the factory was too antiquated. Then he became interested in a steelworks at Bofors, fifty miles or so from Stockholm. Here the factory was more modern and well laid out, though the nearby house which went with it was much more modest than the castle and in disrepair. That setup suited Nobel better than the first one, and he bought the place.

In mid-January, 1894, Nobel told Sohlman and Beckett and the household staff that he was off for London for the cordite hearing. From there he would go on to Sweden, where he would make detailed arrangements for improving and enlarging the Bofors factory. He would try, if possible, to have things in shape before summer.

The weeks in London were extremely painful ones for Alfred Nobel. In a crowded court he claimed — and proved — several highly important basic technical points. Among these was the fact that the opponents' insoluble nitrocellulose could be made soluble. Scientific men were impressed by the extent of Nobel's technical knowledge. The court, too, was impressed — but not convinced. It did not matter that, as Nobel stated, there were many nitrates of cellulose and that nitrocellulose of the same degree of nitration, both soluble and insoluble, could be obtained in ether alcohol. The ballistite patent was limited to soluble nitrocellulose, while the cordite one had used insoluble. Therefore, the court judged, there was no infringement.

The fact that he was treated with great respect did not make the decision any easier for Nobel to take. Nor the public admission that his discovery had been of "revolutionary importance" in the explosives field and had pointed the way to the cordite invention. The lord justice compared the defendants to dwarfs who had climbed on the shoulders of a giant (Nobel) to be able to see farther. Two skillful chemists, he said, had made use of a great invention to obtain practically the same result with only a slight difference in ingredients. That slight difference, however, was enough to warrant the decision, on technical grounds, that the cordite patent was not an infringement on the ballistite patent. And the plaintiff was ordered to pay the entire, very heavy, court costs.

Even if legally correct, this decision struck many of the scientists as harsh. It seemed to Nobel downright unjust. "All the circumstances attending the cordite case affected Nobel deeply," one English scientist who was at the hearing said, "and it is not surprising to find that he considered himself wronged and took it much to heart."

This was an understatement. Alfred Nobel was really crushed by the court's verdict, which he had not expected. He felt that he and his company had been cheated. His sense of justice was deeply offended, and he allowed himself the luxury of bitterness. He was so galled by the lack of appreciation of his work as an inventor that he considered outlining in a letter to the British Government his contribution to the various explosive products they were using and enclosing a bill for one guinea (about five dollars) for his services. His English lawyers talked him out of this, but for a long time he spoke and wrote bitterly to his friends about the "grievous injustice" he had suffered. He tried to work off some of his resentment by writing a sarcastic play, in which he poked fun at the British court system. But the results were not very successful, either in the play or in relieving his feelings. There is no doubt that the cordite case did Nobel real physical harm.

The British Government later arranged with the Nobel Explosives Company to manufacture some cordite. For this, Nobel was paid a sum amounting to about half the royalty he had received for ballistite. So eventually the cordite deal proved to be not quite a total loss to the ballistite inventor or his British company.

Sweden was a happier experience. Alfred Nobel plunged into the remodeling of the Bofors factory, sparing no expense. The people of the district, who had been in a rather bad way since its closing, welcomed the new activity. Nobel had always been a little partial to Swedish workmen, claiming that they were the most honest and honorable men he knew and that they had a particular skill in the explosives field. For a long time most of the Nobel factory managers in the different countries were Swedes. Now at Bofors he had a chance to have practically a full factory roll of Swedes. He installed Robert's eldest son, Hjalmar, as factory manager and, once over-all policies and the general plan of work were established, left things in his hands.

Alfred Nobel was a pioneer in good labor-management relations, though not quite to the extent of Ludwig and Emanuel. He had great respect for the dignity and freedom of even the humblest individual and was always interested in improving factory conditions. He liked to appear unexpectedly in his factories — as if he had come over the back fence, one of his men put it. He would wander about, talking to the workers with almost formal courtesy. Once when he was asked to distribute a certain newspaper in the Bofors factory, he refused. "I should regard it as unreasonable if the workmen at Bofors were to tell me what I should read and not read," he said. "In the same way, they have the right to demand that I shall not make any such interference with their liberties."

As soon as the Bofors factory was ready for action, it began to produce small arms, armorplate, projectiles, and safety explosives. In addition, elaborate experiments in metallurgy and electrochemistry were carried on there. Early the following year, the laboratory beside the factory was completed. It was much larger than the one at San Remo and even more fully equipped. Besides four laboratory workrooms and two workshops, there were separate places for electrolysis experiments, a plant for the manufacture of powder, a place for special apparatus, and a water-gas plant. Nobel sent Ragnar Sohlman up from San Remo to be in charge of the Bofors laboratory and engaged five Swedish chemists to help him. Beckett remained in charge of the laboratory at San Remo.

Nobel's idea was to keep both laboratories going, using the one in the south for the first steps of experiments and then going on with them at the laboratory in the north. Besides planning the projects, he carried in his active brain their underlying principles and the various stages of their progress, as well as many of the details. Sohlman and Beckett kept in close touch by mail and telegraph. Nobel encouraged them and their staffs to start new experiments, checking with him soon and often. This was particularly true in the field of developing civilian products from nitrocellulose.

Nobel was tremendously enthusiastic about Bofors and what could be done there. The factory remodeling had come first, then the building of the laboratory.

Last of all there was the house to be repaired and furnished. It was a big old house at Björkborn, not far
from Bofors. He asked his nephew Hjalmar to take
care of all the details of this. Just so it was ready for
him by the spring of 1895, he would not be fussy about
how it was furnished.

Answering a letter in which Hjalmar evidently had
suggested furnishing one of the guest rooms in a manner suitable for a lady, Nobel amusingly reminded him,
"It is not permissible for a bachelor to have one ladies'
guest room, but he may have several. It might therefore be a good plan to have a few rooms furnished in a
way suitable for ladies and gentlemen of modest requirements. Actually, so far as I have observed, there
is nothing in the construction of the fair — though
usually repulsive — sex to require special furniture."
Nor did he think it was necessary to have a separate
men's smoking room, for "as long as I can afford it I
shall give my men friends good tobacco."

When he stopped off in Paris on his way back to San
Remo after his first summer in Sweden, Alfred Nobel
went to see a doctor. He had been having an increasing amount of discomfort in the neighborhood of his

heart, and the fluctuation of his pulse alarmed him. Although he was inclined to ridicule doctors and their ways, he sometimes consulted them. Now he wrote to his friend Liedbeck, "I have had these rheumatic devils paying a visit to the heart muscles or thereabouts for some days." And he added, "It would be almost a pity if I were to kick the bucket now, because I have some particularly interesting things in hand."

In spite of having reason to be concerned about his health, he treated the matter more lightly than when he was younger, and without the same intense nervous depression. His friends thought his gayer spirits came from his new interests and contacts in Sweden.

That winter of 1894-95, Nobel plunged into new and ambitious experiments at San Remo. Sohlman was still there, and with his help Nobel worked out an improved process for the manufacture of artificial rubber, gutta-percha, and leather, and took out a patent on it. A by-product of this invention was a new type of varnish.

His first English patent in 1895 was on an "improvement in the forging of tubular metallic pieces," and he was soon deep in work on a new kind of "propellant" smokeless powder. The idea of this was to offset the natural tendency of gunpowder to lose power as it leaves a weapon by providing a "progressive consumption" of the powder.

In this "propellant" or "progressive" powder, as in so many other inventions, Nobel started something which others went on with. This was even more true of the many modern industrial products derived from nitrocellulose. Nobel was well on the way to producing a commercially valuable artificial rubber and leather. He also made a real start toward producing artificial silk — rayon — when he invented and patented an extremely fine glass sieve to separate nitrocellulose into the thin filaments of which artificial silk is made. He encouraged a Swedish engineer friend to go a step further and design and patent a machine for manufacturing rayon.

Nobel was never at all grasping or a "dog in the manger" about his ideas. He was more than willing to help others go ahead with inventions that looked hopeful to him and was especially ready to help young inventors without funds.

A young Swedish engineer, Rudolf Lilljequist,

wanted to put up a factory in Sweden for producing chlorine and natron (native carbonate of sodium) from common salt. He had made enough experiments to prove that this could be done commercially, once he had the setup. He knew that Nobel was interested in electrochemistry, so he wrote him in San Remo, early in 1895, explaining his plan. He received a reply from the inventor, saying that he liked the idea and would talk it over with Lilljequist in Stockholm when he came to Sweden that spring. They met, Nobel went over the plan with great care, approved it, and put up a third of the money needed to build the factory and start the company. And the two men became warm personal friends.

Another example of Nobel's help to young inventors was his financing the manufacture of the first bicycle with variable gear, called the Svea velocipede. The two young Swedish brothers who had invented it had no money to manufacture it. Nobel came to their rescue, putting a large sum of money into the formation of a company, the New Cycle Company.

Among other inventions which he helped finance were a special sort of boiler and a silencing device intended to eliminate outside noises from phonographs. This silencing device was an invention which grew out of an idea of his own. Because he was usually ahead of the general scientific knowledge of the time, Nobel was also usually ahead of other inventors. Another reason this frequently happened was that, after getting an idea, he would lose no time in going ahead with experiments and designing apparatus to work it out.

Alfred Nobel went to Sweden in early May of 1895, the first year that both his Bofors factory and laboratory were in operation. The house at Björkborn was ready for him, too, and he was pleased with it. He began to renew old Swedish friendships and to make new ones. He went over to see Robert, who was living a leisurely life on a large estate on the coast. The fertile countryside about Bofors and Björkborn was dotted with sparkling lakes and deep forests. After hours of intense but satisfying work in the laboratory, Nobel would drive about on the country roads, renewing his acquaintance with his native land and delighting in its northern beauty. He had never had a fondness for cities, in spite of living most of his life in them. Now he was happy to have two homes — one north, one south — in quiet, naturally beautiful surroundings. In addition, he still had the Paris house.

The experiments at Bofors, many of which were started at San Remo, were many and varied. Among them, according to Sohlman, were "new kinds of gunpowder, for instance, the so-called progressive powder, explosives and fuses for artillery shells, hot and cold drilling of gun barrels, propulsion charges for rocket projectiles, tightening bands for artillery shells, topographical map-making by means of cameras carried aloft by rockets and then suspended by parachutes, light metal alloys, electrolytic production of potassium and sodium, etc."

That summer of 1895, Nobel was caught up in the general excitement over the daring plans of Salomon August Andrée, a Swedish aeronautical engineer. Andrée wanted to explore the arctic region and to float over the North Pole in a balloon. To do so successfully would be a triumph for Sweden and for air science. It was not so wild an adventure as it sounded, for Andrée was scientifically trained, a longtime student of aeronautics, and an accomplished balloonist. He planned to rig up his balloon with sails and trailing ropes by which he could pretty well control its direction. Already he had made many test flights.

When Andrée had publicized his polar plans earlier that year, he had met with a good deal of ridicule. But Sweden's greatest arctic explorer, Baron Nils Nordenskjold, had believed in the scheme. He had helped Andrée outfit his balloon and enlist a crew. Now money was needed. Nobel's fancy was captured by Andrée's idea. He went to the balloonist and learned more about his plans. Then he promised to supply half the money needed. When this was announced, the balance was pledged by Sweden's King Oscar II and others.

Now that he was in a sense a partner in the expedition, Nobel took great interest in its scientific details. All that summer he worked closely with Andrée, helping plan his equipment and making practical arrangements for it. He also had many conferences with others who were connected with the plan.

One evening Nobel invited Baron Nordenskjold, the Speaker of the Swedish Parliament, and a few other men interested in the Andrée expedition to a dinner in a Stockholm restaurant. The discussion became rather heavy. In an attempt to lighten the serious atmosphere Nobel told a whimsical story of a suicide club where melancholy souls who wanted to depart this life could do so amid soft lights and beautiful music. His guests smiled in a very strained manner. Too late Nobel realized that while the grim fancy, lightly treated, would have been considered humorous in Paris or Vienna, it was too eccentric for matter-of-fact Stockholm!

There were many guests at the Nobel Björkborn house. One of them was no less a personage than the king himself. Oscar II was pleased to honor in this way the famous inventor who had chosen to come back to his native country. Nobel entertained his royal guest handsomely. They talked together of Sweden's newly developing industrialism and of the part the Bofors factory and laboratory could play in it. And they discussed the Andrée expedition. Nobel said he wondered whether Andrée might not find the North Pole deeply indented, due to the rotation of the earth. This idea rather startled the king, who did not know whether or not to take it seriously. When Sohlman heard about the remark later from someone who was present, he declared that Nobel had made it in fun, and that it was just another example of his liking occasionally to say something astonishing, with a perfectly straight face, to see how people would take it.

That fall Alfred Nobel spent two months in Paris, staying there until the middle of December. His heart attacks were more frequent, and he bought himself a sphygmometer to measure his pulse beats and a sphygmograph to record them. He showed the graph to a friend, pointing out the extreme variations. These, he said, were enough to kill a man — and eventually would!

Sitting in his comfortable study in his Paris home, he gave a good deal of thought to what he should do with his fortune. Not one of his relatives needed it. Besides, he believed it was better for a man to make his own way. Any sizable inheritance, he thought, would "encourage laziness and impede the healthy development of the individual's capacity to make an independent position for himself." He looked at the will he had made two years before and decided to change it. He would not let his fortune be nibbled away by leaving almost half of it to relatives, friends, and institutions. He would keep it practically intact and do something big with it for the betterment of mankind and the establishment of peace; something significant. But what — and how?

One idea after another he considered, then discarded. But not for a moment did he consider changing the underlying, basic plan of the earlier will — the awarding of prizes to stimulate and reward successful efforts in the fields of science, literature, and peace. At length, entirely by himself and without any legal advice, he set down briefly and simply the way he wanted his fortune to be used after his death. He had never particularly liked lawyers; since the cordite case he had actively disliked them. This important, intimate task he wanted to do in his own way. When he had the will exactly the way he wanted it, he asked four Swedish friends to meet him at the Swedish Club. Two of them had witnessed the previous will, two years earlier. In their presence, Nobel signed the will and they put down their names as witnesses. The next day Nobel sent the signed document to a bank in Stockholm for safekeeping. He breathed a sigh of relief at having concluded this weighty matter to his satisfaction and went about the business matters he had been postponing for days.

Nobel had never completely given up the idea he had tried, unsuccessfully, to get Aristarchi Bey to work on — getting peace propaganda before the people through their daily newspapers. With this in mind, he had asked his nephew Hjalmar to inquire about the possibility of buying a controlling interest in Stockholm's largest paper. Hjalmar, in his answer, assumed that his uncle wanted the newspaper to promote his own financial interests. Alfred Nobel was indignant at such an idea. "I simply want to own a newspaper in order to rouse or stimulate it to really liberal views," he wrote Hjalmar. "My policy as a newspaper owner would be to use my influence against armaments and such medieval survivals." Nothing, however, came of this idea.

There was not too much sympathy between Alfred Nobel and his nephew Hjalmar. He never could feel for this oldest son of Robert the same warmth he felt for Ludwig's eldest, Emanuel. Yet, always fair, he recognized in Hjalmar a capable engineer and an honest and hard-working factory manager. He regretted Hjalmar's cold ambition and his keener interest in making the factory profitable than in promoting the welfare of its employees. On one occasion Hjalmar suggested that lack of orders seemed to indicate the wisdom of shutting down part of the plant. To this his uncle replied, "In so far as it would involve dismissing any of the workers, I feel we must try to avoid so painful a measure as long as we can."

The winter of 1895-96 was not the active, pleasant one at San Remo which Nobel had anticipated. His heart attacks came oftener and were more severe. Contrary to his usual habit, he called in two doctors. They put him to bed. One of them, he wrote his friend Liedbeck, attributed the trouble to rheumatic gout; the other to gouty rheumatism. Neither of which, he wrote, "is explanation of the fact that my heart pounds like a horse."

He called Sohlman down from Bofors — more, perhaps, to be company for him than in connection with his experimental work in the laboratory. "He is one of the few people I am really fond of," he wrote a friend, and he told another that this fondness was because

Sohlman was "one man who has never asked anything from me."

To ease his pain and forget his misery, Nobel tried again to write. This was something he could do in bed and it was a relief to set down on paper some of the thoughts which raced through his head. He called his play *Nemesis: A Tragedy in Four Acts.* He wrote it in Swedish, in what he called "poetic prose." It was clearly influenced by the English poet Shelley — an influence which had pursued Nobel all his life. Though the few who read it said it was not a very good play, they agreed that there shone out in it his hatred of hypocrisy, ignorance, and fear, and his love of noble living.

Alfred Nobel thought the play was good. He wrote to Bertha von Suttner about it, admitting that he was "curious to see whether this little piece will be played; I feel that on the stage it should be quite effective." He sent it to a Swedish writer he knew, but would not consent to any of the changes she suggested. Neither would he agree to work on it with a collaborator. "I prefer to flutter with my own wings," he wrote, "than to fly with those of others."

Spring came, and the sun shone more warmly on the blue sea stretching southward, on the blossoming mimosa and orange and lemon trees and the gnarled, silver-leaved olives dotting the hillsides. It cheered Alfred Nobel's heart and healed it, at least a little. He got out of bed and out of the house to ride over the awakened countryside and to walk in his fragrant gardens. Soon he was poking his head into the laboratory and then donning his white coat to inspect strange-looking powders, gummy mixtures, and new substances — and to plan new projects.

He gained strength rapidly. Liedbeck came down to see him, and others of his friends. He increased his daily stint of letter writing. And he supervised the furnishing of the next-door villa which had stood empty for almost four years. King Oscar, he thought, might enjoy occupying it if he came south the next winter, as he sometimes did.

A long, full summer at Bofors would be needed, Nobel figured, to make up for the time lost during his winter illness. He would send Sohlman north at once. Not only that, but this year he would have Beckett and his helpers go to Bofors. With a full staff he should be able to make good progress in the electrolysis experiments. There was better equipment for them in the Swedish laboratory than at San Remo. Besides, they could work closely with Lilljequist, whose factory was not too far away.

On the way to Sweden, Nobel made his usual stopover in Paris, then went to London to catch up on business matters there and to visit with some of his English friends. At Bofors, he went at once to the laboratory. He was not feeling so spry as the previous year, he admitted, but the Swedish summer would fix that.

All sorts of research and experimental work went on that season at Bofors. Nobel took out patents for a safety explosive which could be used without danger where there was coal or mining gas, and on an invention designed to measure earth surfaces by a camera "attached to a balloon, rocket, or projectile, and provided with a parachute, as well as with some suitable method for detaching the camera from its vehicle." There were also patents on improvements of previous inventions — inventions concerned with military rockets, progressive powder, motors, armor plating, artillery powder, and artificial silk.

Nobel had not lost his interest in Andrée's polar expedition. He traced its course as it left a Norwegian port and went by boat up the coast to Spitsbergen, where the balloon was to take off. All summer Nobel followed the reports, brought by carrier pigeon, of the progress of the expedition and of the trial flights. In August he, along with many others, was disappointed when news came that Andrée had given up the idea of making the balloon trip over the North Pole that summer, considering it too late in the season to start. He would try again, earlier, the following year.

Sorrow came to Alfred Nobel that same month of August when his oldest brother died. Robert and Alfred, each in poor health for many years, had both outlived the huskier Ludwig. Now Alfred was the only one of his generation left. He took Robert's death to heart and sadly remarked that his turn would come soon. His shoulders sagged and his quick walk grew slow. Friends noticed his disheartened manner and spoke about it among themselves.

He left Bofors in September and went to Paris. At the Swedish Club he talked with some of his friends. He also consulted a noted heart specialist who, Nobel was sure, could diagnose his case better than the two doctors he had had in San Remo the previous winter. As he feared, the physician told him that his heart disease — hardening of the aorta — was very serious. He must stop his hard work and take it easy.

"This does not mean that I must be idle," Nobel wrote Liedbeck, "but only that I must as far as possible avoid strenuous traveling." He wrote Sohlman that he would be in Paris awhile, until the specialist could determine the best method of treatment. And he added, "It seems an irony of fate that they should be prescribing nitroglycerin internally for me! They call it trinktin, to avoid terrifying the chemists [druggists] and the public."

A month later Nobel was still in Paris, and he wrote this letter to Bertha von Suttner:

Dear Baroness and Friend:
"Feeling well" — no, unhappily for me, I am not, and I am even consulting doctors, which is contrary not only to my custom, but also to my principles. I, who have no heart, figuratively speaking, have one organically, and I am conscious of it. But that will suffice for me and my petty miseries. I am enchanted to see that the peace move-

ment is gaining ground. That is due to the civilizing of the masses, and especially to the prejudice hunters and darkness hunters, among whom you hold an exalted rank. Those are your titles of nobility.

Heartily yours,

A. NOBEL

Later, on the day he wrote the baroness, Nobel left for San Remo. He was glad to be back in that warm, pleasant place. He wrote to Sohlman in Bofors that he was feeling comparatively well, and spoke of various research and experiments, and of the preparations to be made for Andrée's postponed expedition the next summer.

On December 7, he wrote Sohlman again:

The samples you have sent are particularly good. The pure nitrocellulose powder seems to me to be splendid. Unfortunately my health is so bad again that it is difficult for me to write even these few lines, but as soon as I am able I shall return to the matters which interest us.

Your devoted friend,

A. NOBEL

Alfred Nobel never returned to his laboratory. Within hours of writing the letter he was taken critically ill. His faithful servants carried him from his study to his bedroom upstairs and called a doctor. He directed them to keep Nobel in bed and as quiet as possible. They found this hard to do, as he was extremely restless. He talked a little in Swedish, the language of his childhood, which none of them could understand. Nor did he seem to understand them when they spoke in French or in Italian. Auguste, the old French butler, felt sure that Nobel wanted word sent to his family. So Auguste sent three telegrams: to Emanuel Nobel in Russia; to Hjalmar Nobel in Sweden; and to Ragnar Sohlman, also in Sweden.

When Ragnar Sohlman received the telegram he was filled with compassion. He thought of this gentle man — his employer but also his friend — lying alone in his Italian villa, desperately ill, with only his servants near him. He remembered that Nobel had once expressed the fear that this very thing would happen to him. At that time he had spoken of his natural longing for "a close friend or relation whose kind hand would some day close one's eyes and whisper in one's ear a gentle and sincere word of comfort." Ragnar Sohlman determined to go to San Remo as speedily as possible to give whatever help and comfort he could to his friend in his critical illness.

Hjalmar Nobel also decided to go to San Remo. He and Sohlman met on the way and finished the journey together. Near its end they received a telegram, sent by Emanuel Nobel, who had arrived in San Remo earlier that tenth day of December, 1896. The telegram informed them of his uncle's death very early that morning. Emanuel had also arrived too late. Alfred Nobel had died as he had lived — alone.

They had a simple funeral service at Villa Mio Nido. For it, Emanuel Nobel invited his uncle's friend, Nathan Söderblom, pastor of the Swedish Church in Paris, to come and deliver a short address. From San Remo the body would be taken to Stockholm for a more formal service in Storkyrka, the great and ancient Swedish church, and from there a solemn procession would escort it to the cemetery where Alfred Nobel's father, mother, and brother Emil were buried.

In his "eloquent and dignified" address Dr. Söderblom said, "It was a natural corollary of the loneliness and suffering that were his lot, that in the public estimation he should have figured too much as a rich and remarkable man, too little as a human being. Let us not perpetuate this error now that he is dead. . . . His was not a nature to be hardened by money or success, or to be embittered by loneliness; to the end of his life he was warmhearted and kind." And, with no thought of an English pun on Alfred Nobel's name, the pastor added, "In the life beyond, all that matters is to have lived nobly."

II

Creating
the Nobel
Foundation

MOST BIOGRAPHIES end with the death of the man or woman, for most persons' vital impact on others ends there. But Alfred Nobel's vital impact on others did not end with his death, and so his story cannot end there either. The reason for Alfred Nobel's continuing and increasing influence was the will, the remarkable will that he made in Paris a year before his death.

Ragnar Sohlman was already in bed on the evening of December 15 when Emanuel and Hjalmar Nobel came to his room. They told him that they had just received a telegram from Stockholm. Their uncle's will had been opened at the bank where it had been held in safekeeping. It named Ragnar Sohlman as one of the two executors of the will; Rudolf Lilljequist was the other.

That night Ragnar Sohlman tossed and turned and could not sleep. Why, he asked himself, had he — a young chemical research engineer — been chosen to execute what must be an important will? He had no training or experience at all to qualify him for such a task. And he had not even met the man he was to work with. Why hadn't Alfred Nobel chosen Emanuel, the eldest and closest of his nephews and a thoroughly dependable, accomplished businessman? Or his old friend Alarik Liedbeck? The only two reasons Sohlman could imagine he was named were that he had no personal interest in the will, and that Nobel knew he would follow his employer's directions faithfully and carefully. Nothing and no one, Ragnar Sohlman resolved that night, should keep him from doing this.

The day after the funeral service a letter arrived from Stockholm with a copy of the will. It was a complete surprise to Emanuel Nobel, to Hjalmar Nobel, and to Ragnar Sohlman — and not a happy one. Each of them read and reread it. A few minor gifts and then:

The whole of my remaining realizable estate shall be dealt with in the following way:

The capital shall be invested by my executors in safe securities and shall constitute a fund, the interest on which shall be annually distributed in the form of prizes to those who, during the preceding year, shall have conferred the greatest benefit on mankind. The said interest shall be divided into five equal parts, which shall be apportioned as follows: one part to the person who shall have made the most important discovery or invention within the field of physics; one part to the person who shall have made the most important chemical discovery or improvement; one part to the person who shall have made the most important discovery within the domain of physiology or medicine; one part to the person who shall have produced in the field of literature the most outstanding work of an idealistic tendency; and one part to the person who shall have done the most or the best work for fraternity among nations, for the abolition or reduction of standing armies and for the holding and promotion of peace congresses.

The prizes for physics and chemistry shall be awarded by the Swedish Academy of Science; that for physiological or medical works by the Caroline Institute in Stockholm; that for literature by the Academy in Stockholm; and that for champions of peace by a committee of five persons to be elected by the Norwegian Storting. It is my express wish that in awarding the prizes no consideration whatever shall be given to the nationality of the candidates, so that the most worthy shall receive the prize, whether he be a Scandinavian or not.

ALFRED BERNHARD NOBEL

Paris, November 27, 1895

Among his uncle's papers Emanuel Nobel had found the will of 1893, in which he was named as one of the executors. In it the bequests to him and to other members of the Nobel family were much larger than in the later will. Emanuel was disturbed, too, that the Nobel Brothers' Naphtha Company of Baku was not mentioned in the final will, although his uncle had held a controlling interest in it. Hjalmar was disappointed in the will both personally and because there was no provision in it for the continuation of the Bofors factory. And Ragnar Sohlman was distressed that it did not provide for his going on at the Bofors laboratory with the technical experiments which were progressing so favorably.

For a time these considerations overshadowed in their minds the real significance of the will. Apparently they continued to do so with Hjalmar Nobel. But Emanuel Nobel and Ragnar Sohlman had several long,

earnest talks, in which they reasoned together as to
what lay behind the will in its maker's mind. They told
each other of conversations with Alfred Nobel in
which he had spoken of his desire to do something to
help in the advance of science and the promotion of
peace. They spoke of his idealism and his lofty goals.
Emanuel Nobel mentioned his own responsibility, as
the oldest of Alfred Nobel's brothers' children, for
the financial interests of the others. Yet, he said, he
considered observing his uncle's wishes an even higher
responsibility.

In every way Emanuel Nobel's attitude toward the
younger man was "highminded and courteous," according to Ragnar Sohlman himself. "You must always
remember," he told him, "the obligation implied in
the Russian word for the executor of a will — *Dushe
Prikashshik* — which means 'the spokesman for the
soul.' You must try to act accordingly."

Hjalmar left for Sweden. Emanuel Nobel and Ragnar Sohlman remained in San Remo long enough to
put things in order and close Mio Nido. Then they
made the long journey to Stockholm together.

The responsibility which had been dropped upon

young Sohlman so unexpectedly weighed heavily on him. He had respected his employer greatly. He had also been very fond of him. He kept thinking back with pity to the last days of the man — alone, except for his Italian doctor and his French servants, none of whom was able to understand a single one of his final words. Saddened and deeply depressed, Sohlman resolved again that to the best of his ability he would carry out his employer's wishes as expressed so simply in his will. As he pondered over those wishes, the originality and grandeur of Alfred Nobel's idea began to dawn upon him, and he thought deeply about the idea and about the man who had created it. Who but a true idealist would have dreamed up such a plan? Who but a strong believer in the power of science and culture to raise mankind to heights of worthy peaceful living? For the first time Ragnar Sohlman felt not only devotion toward the task ahead but enthusiasm for it.

Soon after the Stockholm funeral Alfred Nobel's will was made public. It created a sensation. People were dumfounded to learn that practically the whole estate of eight or nine million dollars — a huge fortune then — was to be put into a fund whose income was to go as prizes to benefactors of the human race. The leading Swedish newspaper declared that this "gift to mankind, intended to further its development and promote its welfare, as well as to serve purely idealistic purposes . . . was probably the most magnificent one of its kind that a private person has ever had both the desire and the ability to make."

Not everyone agreed. There were some bitter remarks about this man who cared more for the human race than for his relatives; this Swede who favored international activities above Swedish institutions and interests. Why should he expect Swedish organizations to act as caretakers of his fortune and awarders of his prizes? Most of all, why had he, a Swede, chosen a committee of the Norwegian parliament to select a peace prize winner?

There was much bad blood between Sweden and Norway just at that moment. Although Norway was to all purposes self-governing, there was a "union" between it and Sweden, and this union was distasteful to many Norwegians and many Swedes. Defenders of the will explained Nobel's turning to Norway as the selector of the peace prize winner on the grounds of

Norway's long record as a peaceful and peace-loving nation, its geographical location, which tended to keep it neutral in time of war, and its positive stand in favor of international arbitration. Perhaps, they said, he thought this gesture would help ease the strained relations between the two countries.

Early in January, 1897, the two executors of the Nobel will met for the first time. Ragnar Sohlman was relieved to find Rudolf Lilljequist a realistic, experienced businessman several years older than himself and without any personal ax to grind. The two men worked together harmoniously, each respecting the other's character and opinions. Since neither of them knew much about court formalities and legal procedures, their first move was to employ expert lawyers. Carl Lindhagen, a Swedish deputy justice who was later mayor of Stockholm, became their principal attorney and a great help in solving the problems involved in carrying out Nobel's wishes. For there were problems — big ones.

In the first place, Hjalmar Nobel and his mother and brother and sister were determined to try to have the will changed. They had expected to receive more of Alfred Nobel's money, and thought they should.

Then there was the matter of establishing Nobel's legal residence. Under the laws of which country should the will be executed — Sweden, France, or Italy? He had lived in all three countries and had owned his home in each one.

Although the purpose of the will was clear, it did not state who was to administer the money. Should a body be set up to handle the fund? How should this be done? Would the various institutions mentioned in the will all agree to act as selectors of the prize winners in their particular field? What rules and regulations should guide them? How much power did the executors have to make necessary changes in the will? And how should they handle the tremendous task of turning all Nobel's financial assets into "safe securities"?

Lilljequist was busy building a new electrochemical factory and could not very well leave the country. And so the two executors agreed that he should take care of matters in Sweden while Sohlman handled matters in other countries.

Sohlman's first trip was to Norway. There he found

the president of the Norwegian Storting, or parliament, and several of its leading members favorably inclined toward taking on the task of selecting the Nobel peace prize winners.

In Paris, Sohlman called on the Swedish-Norwegian minister and on Herre Nordling, the Swedish consul general, and engaged a French lawyer and a notary to make an inventory of the Nobel French holdings. Sohlman soon discovered that if the Nobel legal residence were considered to be Paris, and if French courts handled the will, the taxes would be extremely high and would be on everything held by Nobel in all countries. Sohlman discovered also that because of its informality the will might be thrown out by a French court, which would put Robert Nobel's family in a strong position to break it.

From every angle it seemed both right and best to have the will probated in Sweden. Sohlman was sure that Nobel, in spite of his frequent quip, "My home is where I work, and I work everywhere," had considered himself a Swede. He had written his will in Swedish, had it witnessed by four Swedes, and had appointed two other Swedes as executors. And he had chosen Swedish or Norwegian institutions to select his prize winners. Surely Alfred Nobel had thought of Sweden as his real home.

Herre Nordling legally vouched for Sohlman, so that he could dispose of the Nobel assets in France. Emanuel Nobel came to Paris to see Sohlman about the Nobel Baku company shares. If they were sold quickly, in one lot, the value of all the Baku stock would go way down. Some of the stockholders thought Emanuel Nobel should try to prevent this by contesting the will. When Sohlman pledged that, as executor, he would not permit a forced sale of the oil stock, Emanuel Nobel promised to support the will, as he personally wanted to do. But he warned that there would be trouble with the Swedish Nobels.

Sohlman wrote to Hjalmar and Ludwig Nobel, urging them to honor their uncle's will. When they would not agree to do this, Sohlman asked Herre Lindhagen, the Swedish lawyer, to come to Paris. Lindhagen, Sohlman, and Nordling decided to withdraw all the Nobel securities from the different French banks and business firms where they were and get them together in one place, ready to send out of France in a hurry, if necessary. They did this slowly, over three weeks' time, in order not to attract attention. Then Sohlman went to London, engaged an English lawyer, and made arrangements at a bank for the French securities to be received, stored, and eventually sold there.

From London, Sohlman went on to Sweden for the hearing on the will, which had been submitted for probate. The newspapers made a great deal of the hearing. Many of them doubted the legality of the will; others doubted its wisdom. All this publicity made the Robert Nobel family even more antagonistic.

A telegram from Nordling in Paris informed Sohlman that Hjalmar and Ludwig Nobel and their sister's husband were there, that they had hired a French lawyer and were trying to get French court action against the will.

There was no time to lose. Sohlman hurried back to Paris. His lawyers and Nordling and he agreed that the Nobel securities must be spirited out of France — fast. The ones to be sold should go to London; the ones to be held as "safe securities" for the estate should go to Stockholm. But how could this be done so it would not attract attention? Any knowledge of the move might mean robbery attempts or a court injunction by the relatives — or both.

Sohlman and his advisers decided it would be too obvious for a bank to handle the transfer and too risky for him to carry the valuable securities personally to London and Stockholm. They agreed that they would send out one package a day by the French equivalent of the Railway Express, insuring it with the post office and a banking firm for the maximum amount possible under the circumstances.

Each morning for a week Nordling, Sohlman, and a trusted clerk brought from Stockholm took a bunch of the valuable papers out of the strongboxes, put them into an ordinary suitcase, and carried them by horse cab to the consul general's office. There they sorted and listed the securities, tied them into small packages, wrapped and sealed them. Then they put them back into the suitcase and, in the afternoon, took them to the railway station, again using a horse cab. Of these rides Sohlman wrote, "With a loaded revolver in my hand I sat in the cab prepared to defend the suitcase in case a collision with another carriage had been arranged by robbers — at that time a not un-usual occurrence in Paris."

Nothing like this happened. But one day, when Sohlman and the trusted clerk were listing the securi-ties in an inner room at the consul general's office, who should appear in the reception room but the three Swedish relatives! As they discussed the will with the consul general, they had no idea of what was going on in the next room. But their visit made Nordling worry about having helped the executors, because he knew that, as a representative of Sweden, he should be completely objective. The Swedish attorney tried to ease his mind. All he had been guilty of, Lindhagen said, was "aiding, as a conscientious Swedish official should, in the accomplishment of Nobel's commend-able purposes."

But Nordling continued to feel that he was in a bad position. As soon as the last of the securities were on their way to London and Stockholm he proposed that they all get together with the relatives at a "peace and reconciliation" dinner. Sohlman did not much like the idea, but he could not very well refuse.

Nordling arranged an elaborate dinner at a famous

French restaurant. Everyone came. The atmosphere was rather chilly at first, but with the fine food and wines it began to grow brighter. By the time coffee arrived, Nordling felt they could safely begin to discuss the ticklish situation.

"Why," Hjalmar Nobel asked Ragnar Sohlman, "are you pretending that Sweden was my uncle's legal home? That is ridiculous! Paris was his real residence, and a French court is the proper court to decide on his will."

"That," replied Sohlman calmly, "is perhaps open to discussion. But it is not too important, since practically none of the securities would come under the authority of the French courts."

"Why not?" Hjalmar wanted to know.

"Because they are no longer in Paris," Sohlman told him.

At first Hjalmar refused to believe this, but when Nordling said it was so, he had to accept the fact.

"If you still insist on contesting the will," Sohlman said, "I would advise your doing so in Sweden rather than in France."

Hjalmar muttered something about the possibility

of arbitration but did not suggest anything definite. Soon the dinner gathering broke up. Instead of having been a "peace and reconciliation" meeting, it had turned out to be quite the opposite.

The Swedish relatives' French lawyers were extremely annoyed with themselves for not having taken action earlier to hold Nobel's assets in France. The furniture and furnishings and personal belongings at the Nobel Paris house had already been sold at auction, but not the house. The lawyers secured a court attachment which stopped its sale. This caused quite a loss to the estate and did not help the relatives' cause at all. Because, months later, a French court — as well as a Swedish court — ruled that Alfred Nobel's legal residence at the time of his death was Bofors, Sweden.

Hjalmar Nobel tried to make trouble for the executors in Germany and in England, as well as in Sweden. But public sentiment was turning against him. This was partly due to the Swedish attorney general's recommendation that the Swedish Government do what it could to help put Nobel's "noble intentions into effect," and the government's direction to him and to the Swedish institutions involved to take whatever legal steps were necessary to do this.

Long before, those institutions, as well as the Norwegian Storting, had been formally requested by the executors to assume the responsibilities mentioned in the will. The Norwegian parliament was the first to reply; it accepted the responsibility of administering the peace prize. Some of the Swedish institutions were afraid that the new duties would take too much time from their already full programs, but after much discussion all the institutions officially accepted their role of prize-winner selector except the Academy of Science. This institution, which was to choose both the physics and chemistry prize winners, refused to act until the will had been legally proved. And to prove the will, *all* the prize-winner-selecting institutions must have accepted their responsibilities. So there was a deadlock which seemed to necessitate a compromise with the relatives.

The two executors decided to call to Stockholm the lawyers from Germany, France, and England. With the Swedish lawyer, they had a truly international little conference. Each lawyer expressed his opinions and, outside the meetings, discussed with the executors the special problems facing him in his country. It was decided to delay any possible compromise with the relatives until the full inventory of the estate had been completed.

At the time of Alfred Nobel's death no one had thought to inform the Baroness von Suttner of it. She read the news in a paper and was saddened by this abrupt end of "the tie of a twenty years' friendship." She was also curious as to whether her friend had remembered his pledge to "do something great" for the peace movement. When, later, she read that Alfred Nobel's fortune had been left "for benevolent purposes, a part to go toward promoting the peace movement," she felt she must know more. She wrote to the Austrian ambassador to Sweden, in Stockholm, who sent her a copy of the will. Then Sohlman wrote her, telling her of the efforts of the Swedish Nobels to break the will, of Emanuel Nobel's determination to support it, and of the fear of some conservative Swedes that the Norwegian Government might misuse its power as awarder of the peace prize.

There was nothing Bertha von Suttner or any other

of the "champions of peace" could do but wait. Meantime they rejoiced with one another over this action which had brought so much attention to their cause. "It has been openly declared to the world," the baroness wrote, "not by an overexcited dreamer, but by an inventor of genius (an inventor of war material into the bargain), that the brotherhood of nations, the diminution of armies, the promotion of Peace Congresses, belong to the things that signify most for the well-being of mankind."

By fall, that year of 1897, the assets in the different countries were finally listed and evaluated. There was most in France, the next largest amount in Germany (where some of the Russian securities were held), then came Sweden, Russia, Scotland, and England, with smaller amounts in Italy, Austria, and Norway. The entire estate came to nearly nine million dollars — one of the largest fortunes, the papers said, to have been accumulated by a single man of business. The taxes to be paid to the various governments amounted to close to ten per cent of the amount.

In December, after a trip to London and Hamburg, Ragnar Sohlman accepted an invitation from Emanuel

Nobel to spend a few days with him in St. Petersburg. They discussed the will and worked out a way of transferring the Baku oil shares to Emanuel Nobel for the Nobel family.

During January and February, 1898, official representatives of the Swedish Academy and the Caroline Medical-Surgical Institute met together several times, joined unofficially by representatives of the non-cooperating Academy of Science. They discussed setting up an over-all organization to be called the Nobel Foundation.

Emanuel Nobel came from St. Petersburg to attend some of the meetings. Before he left Russia, he called his relatives together and asked their approval of the attitude which he wanted to take toward his uncle's will. Supporting it might mean less money for them, he explained, but he felt it would mean more honor. Without exception, every member of the Russian branch of the Nobel family encouraged him to stand by the will.

The conference representatives knew that Emanuel Nobel represented the family of Ludwig Nobel, the Russian branch of the Nobel family, with eight of the twenty legal heirs of Alfred Nobel. It was common knowledge that there was some rivalry between the Russian and the Swedish Nobels because of the Baku oil wells. The children of Robert Nobel thought that the prosperity of the Nobel Brothers' Naphtha Company was due to Robert's discovery and early development of the wells. The children of Ludwig Nobel believed that it was first Ludwig's ability, work, and money, and then Emanuel's, that had made the Baku oil business so important.

For a time at the meetings Emanuel Nobel only listened. Then he spoke, saying that he wished to respect his uncle's wishes and that he did not intend to dispute the terms of the will. It was clear, however, that some changes and additions must be made in it if those wishes were to be fulfilled. He would like this group to inform him of whatever changes or additions they proposed, so that he could consider them for himself and for those whom he represented. The institutional representatives gladly promised this.

Emanuel Nobel's statement had been courageous. Not only had his Swedish cousins urged him to join with them in their effort to break the will, but the

Swedish king had summoned him to discuss the matter. King Oscar personally thought Alfred Nobel's will fantastically idealistic, as well as impossibly difficult to administer. In addition, he disliked Norway's connection with it. He suggested to Emanuel Nobel that it was his duty to protect the financial interests of his family. To this Emanuel replied, "Your Majesty, I would not care to expose my sisters and brothers to the risk of being reproached, in the future, by distinguished scientists for having appropriated funds which properly belong to them." (When Emanuel's Russian lawyer heard of this, he begged him to leave Sweden immediately. For who knew what might happen to a man who dared to speak so freely to a king!)

Emanuel Nobel's public statement supporting his uncle's will made it more difficult for the twelve members of Robert Nobel's family to go on with their opposition. They did bring suit against the executors, but at the hearing they stated that if they won their case, they would carry out the main intentions of the will.

Public opinion was gradually becoming more favorable toward the idea of the will. Never mind, the peo-

ple said now, if it was extraordinary. Alfred Nobel had
been the first Swede to make so much money and they
were proud of him. Perhaps he was ahead of his times
in thinking that a great fortune was not merely a family affair but "a trust to be put into service for public
benefit." Perhaps, after all, a fortune dedicated to
such "idealistic and international purposes" would
bring credit and honor to Sweden. Conservative members of the Swedish Government who had been
doubtful about the whole thing became openly favorable. The Academy of Science changed its attitude
and sent an official representative to the foundation-
planning sessions. And eventually the king became
the loyal supporter of the Nobel Foundation, even
agreeing to take a personal part in its ceremonies.

Chiefly because of Emanuel Nobel's influence, it
was possible to settle out of court the lawsuit started
by the Swedish relatives. In return for dropping the
suit, they were given a year's interest on the estate in
addition to the sum they would get in any case, under
Swedish law. And at their request they were represented at the sessions which decided on the statutes
of the Nobel Foundation.

Now, almost two years after the death of Alfred Nobel, the worst of the drawn-out battle of the will was over. There were still many details to be worked out as to how the prize winners would be chosen, but the statutes of the Nobel Foundation had been drawn up and approved by all concerned, including the Swedish Government.

The money was ready. Alfred Nobel's assets in different countries had been turned into "safe securities." The San Remo house had been sold to a German friend of Nobel's; the houses at Paris and at Björkborn had been sold at public auction. The laboratory at Bofors was to go on for one year, and also the work of the various inventors whose research Nobel had been financing. His library at the Paris house and the one at San Remo, as well as papers and correspondence relating to inventions or other subjects of interest, were to be placed in a Nobel Trust to be made available to students.

By the time the twentieth century came in, everything was in readiness to put into action the great idea of this nineteenth-century man with a twentieth-century mind.

12

Lengthening
Shadows

"I HAVE A DESIRE," Alfred Nobel told one of the Swedish engineers who witnessed his will in the Paris Swedish Club in November, 1895, "to create a spiritual family which, down through the ages, shall be enabled to give their best services to humanity through the agency of my money."

Alfred Nobel thought that in his will he had adequately charted the course for this desire — a desire so lofty and idealistic that the king of Sweden called it "fantastic." Nobel had stated his idea in the same broad terms he used when he laid out one of his long-range projects for an assistant to work on. He seldom gave detailed instructions when he entrusted persons with responsible jobs. Not if he had confidence in them. And he had the greatest confidence in the two executors of his will, Rudolf Lilljequist and Ragnar Sohlman.

It was thanks to them, and especially to the devotion and persistence of Ragnar Sohlman — and the loyalty of Emanuel Nobel — that the too-simple will survived the rough seas of legal technicalities and hostile opposition. It was their work that brought the Nobel Foundation into being.

On a rocky knoll near the Stockholm observatory a building was set up to provide a place for the work of carrying out Alfred Nobel's long-reaching desire. Here the five persons who made up the managing board of the Nobel Foundation would meet to administer the huge funds for which they were responsible and the other affairs of the foundation. The Swedish Government had appointed the president of the board, and each of the Swedish prize-awarding institutions had selected one of its members. Each institution also had three trustees, except the Swedish Academy, which had six, since it was responsible for awarding two prizes. Each institution also had a Nobel

Committee of from three to five members to help investigate proposed prize winners. In addition, the institutions had the right, according to the statutes of the foundation, to set up scientific institutions or other such related organizations, to be known as Nobel Institutes.

One fourth of the income from the main fund was to be used for expenses and for the administration of the foundation and the institutes. Three fourths of the income was to be given, in five equal amounts, as prizes. These amounts would vary from year to year according to the income from the fund and the varying tax rates, but the amount of each prize would never fall lower, it was thought, than a sum equal to thirty thousand dollars and might more usually be a sum equal to around forty thousand. In case some years a prize was not given, that money would go back into the main fund, or it might go into a special fund "to be used to further the testator's ultimate purpose in other ways than by prize awards."

The trustees of the Nobel Foundation met for the first time on September 25, 1900, and the board a week later. A little over a year from then, on the fifth anniversary of Alfred Nobel's death, December 10, 1901, the first prizes were awarded. Four of the five prizes — those for chemistry, physics, physiology and medicine, and literature — were given in Stockholm; the prize for peace was given in Oslo, then known as Christiania.

The day of the awarding of the prizes was a great one in both cities. The ceremony was so carefully planned that it would be followed with little change for more than half a century. In Stockholm, it took place in the Royal Academy of Music, one of the city's largest, loveliest halls. The great place was adorned with emblems and flowers, and in the place of honor stood a bust of Alfred Nobel.

Though later held in the afternoon, that first ceremony was set for seven in the evening. Invited guests arrived early, dressed in their best. The royal orchestra played soft music. Members of the Swedish cabinet, ministers of foreign countries, and members of various diplomatic corps came in, wearing their colorful ribbons and orders and medals and escorting their ladies glistening in silks and satins and velvets and aglitter with jewels. A hush, then gaily dressed heralds appeared and sounded a fanfare on their silver trumpets. The audience rose as, preceded by their guard of honor, the royal family came slowly down the aisle. They stood before their seats at the front of the great hall while a choir sang the Swedish national anthem. Then the royal party and the audience seated themselves and the orchestra played again.

Soon there was another pause and silence as the heralds again lifted their silver trumpets. This time they stood at the back of the broad stage. At the sound of the second fanfare doors opened to let onto the stage trustees and board members of the Nobel Foundation and members of the various committees, then the winners of the first Nobel prizes. Three of the four were present that first year; the minister of his country received the award for the fourth. Present also were Emanuel Nobel and other representatives of the Nobel family.

The audience had stood as these dignitaries took their places on the platform, facing the royal family and close to five thousand persons. Now everyone was seated, and a chorus of men's voices sang, and the president of the foundation delivered a brief address.

And then, with musical numbers by the orchestra and various choruses interspersed, the prize winners were introduced and the prizes awarded. The prince royal, Prince Eugene, presented them — to each winner an envelope containing a check for a sum equal to forty thousand five hundred dollars, and a gold medallion bearing an engraved likeness of Alfred Nobel and an inscription. The dignified ceremony ended with the chanting of the Swedish national hymn beginning, *"Du gamla, du fria, du fjällhöga Nord"* — Thou ancient, unconquered, rockbound Northland.

That first year the prize winners were a distinguished group. From Germany the famous physician Wilhelm Konrad Röntgen had come to receive the physics prize for the discovery of the new rays which he called X rays and which others called by his name. The chemistry prize was won by Jacobus Hendricus van't Hoff, a Dutch research chemist who had founded a new branch of science, stereochemistry, which dealt with the arrangement and measuring of molecules, and who discovered the law of chemical dynamics. The German doctor-bacteriologist Emil von Behring received the physiology and medicine prize for his development of a serum effective against diphtheria. "He placed in the hands of the physician a victorious weapon against illness and death," the official announcement stated. First to win the Nobel prize in literature was a French poet, Sully Prudhomme. He was not able to be present; the minister of France to Sweden accepted the prize for him.

The prize winners were given the keys to the city of Stockholm and entertained in truly royal fashion. Besides the formal presentation ceremony they had dinner with the king at his palace and were the guests of honor at a great banquet at which the crown prince presided. Formal toasts were offered to the king, to the memory of Alfred Nobel, and to the candidates. Within the week following the presentation ceremony, the prize winners delivered the lectures on their subjects which their acceptance of the prizes obligated them to prepare, unless circumstances compelled a later date.

Meantime, in Christiania, the peace prize was awarded in a solemn ceremony in the Norwegian Storting, or parliament. The checks came from the same Stockholm bank on which the other four checks were drawn; otherwise all arrangements were made in the Norwegian capital.

This gathering was held in the morning, at an extraordinary session of the parliament. Prince Karl and Princess Ingeborg of Sweden's ruling family were present, members of the Norwegian cabinet, the diplomatic corps, officials of the Nobel Institute and committees, and invited guests. In later years, after the Nobel Institute had its own building, the ceremony was held in its assembly hall.

The peace prize winners — there were two the first year — were announced by the Storting president; the Swedish prince presented the checks and medals. The honored men were Jean Henri Dunant, the Swiss founder of the Red Cross and originator of the Geneva Convention, and Frédéric Passy, French peace pioneer and president of the French Society for Arbitration Between Nations. Dunant was unable to be present and a member of the Nobel Committee received the award for him.

The winners had been determined after much consideration and long debate. Candidates for the other prizes could be recommended by anyone in the special field "with the competence therefor." Not so the peace prize. The privilege of making nominations for it was confined to members of the parliament of Norway and the governments of other nations, members of the Interparliamentary Union, advisers to the Nobel Institute, and university professors of history, law, and political science.

The awarding of the first Nobel prizes made a tremendous stir all over the Western world. Of course there were criticisms, both of the prize winners chosen and of some of the principles which had seemed to influence their selection.

One criticism, heard both that first year and in many later years, was that the prizes went mostly to older persons who had accomplished their lifework rather than, as Alfred Nobel had hoped, placing "those whose work showed promise in a position of such complete independence that they would be able to devote their whole energies to their work." His friends remembered his desire "to encourage great minds to continued activity in the service of humanity."

Sometimes, through the years, this has happened.

Fridtjof Nansen, wanting badly to get back to his scientific research on arctic exploration, stuck to his job of placing prisoners of war and finding homes for refugees after the First World War. Because, he said, "this great reward binds me fast to the work I have begun."

But in his will Nobel had clearly stated that the prizes should go "to those persons who during the previous year have rendered the greatest service to mankind." The prize awarders, bound by these words, have most often given the Nobel prizes as a crowning reward for a noble achievement in science, literature, or the promotion of peace.

The phrase "the previous year" has been a difficult one for prize selectors to apply. It cannot be taken too literally, for often an experiment which comes to a conclusion, or a discovery which is made, in one year is the result of many years' work. Its "service to mankind," too, may not be proved beyond doubt for several years.

Another of Alfred Nobel's statements which critics have brought up is this: "I would not leave anything to a man of action, as he would be tempted to give up

work. On the other hand, I would like to help dreamers, as they find it difficult to get on in life." But how
could those who recommended candidates know
which were the talented dreamers? And even if
known, would they be eligible under the terms of the
will? It stated explicitly persons who already had "conferred the greatest benefit on mankind."

Neither can the prizes be given on the basis of need.
Many times a prize has gone to a person who has had
no real need for the money. But that person had earned
the prize. Frequently such a winner has used the
money to help younger persons or to accomplish something he or she felt was in line with Alfred Nobel's
desires.

Those first prize winners were proud of the honor
they received in the name of Alfred Nobel. The prize
winners who have followed them, year after year, have
received their honor with even more pride. For the
Nobel prizes have increased in importance and influence until they have come to be considered "the high-
est scientific distinction in the whole world." Welcome
though the money award has often been to a winner,
probably never has it outweighed the honor of be-

coming a Nobel prize winner. No other prizes have brought such fame to the winners.

Turning things about, no other list of prize winners has done such credit to the prizes. The list of Nobel prize winners reads like an international roll of honor. Among the scientists following Röntgen have come the Curies, Marconi, Einstein, Carrel, Compton, and Urey; among the writers, Kipling, Maeterlinck, Tagore, Yeats, Shaw, Mann, and Eugene O'Neill; among the "champions of peace," Bertha von Suttner, Nansen, Woodrow Wilson, Jane Addams, Schweitzer, Bunche, and Pearson.

Alfred Nobel's shadow is a lengthening one. Each year, the interest in the prizes is greater than the year before. Press representatives go to Sweden and Norway from many countries, and the December tenth ceremonies are reported in all leading papers and news periodicals. Many who read these reports do not, after half a century, quite remember what it was that Alfred Nobel invented. Yet his name is not forgotten in the worlds of science and industry.

When, considerably more than twenty years after Nobel's death, executives changed the name of the

Nobel Explosives Company, omitting Nobel's name, "it was found that the name Nobel was a title of nobility in the world of industry, and constituted an historical asset not lightly to be dispensed with; the name of the trust was accordingly changed to Nobel Industries, Ltd."

In the summer of 1957, people's memories were jogged as honor was indirectly paid to Nobel the scientist when an international team of scientists produced a new element, number 102, and named it nobelium. It was a truly international achievement, with the United States Argonne National Laboratory providing rare isotopes of curium (element number 96), the British Atomic Energy Research Establishment providing the rare isotope of carbon to bombard the curium, and the Nobel Institute for Physics in Sweden furnishing the powerful cyclotron to do the bombarding job. Nobelium was named for the laboratory where the work was done, and a science periodical reminded its readers that the Nobel Institute for Physics "was named in honor of the Swedish chemist, the late Alfred Nobel, who established the Nobel Prizes awarded for outstanding contributions in the arts and sciences." Although nobelium existed a few months after its discovery only in the laboratory, one of its discoverers declared, "You never know where these things may lead. The discovery of aluminum meant nothing for a long time."

Though linked to science, Nobel's name is most often connected with his prizes. Each year through them he stimulates and rewards the widening of knowledge and of brotherhood, and directs the attention of people everywhere to achievements in science, literature, and peace. And so Alfred Nobel makes his continuing contribution to the advancement of mankind, and in doing so, the shadow of the man lengthens.

Other shadows also lengthen. Alfred Nobel thought that if war were not abolished within thirty years the world would "inevitably relapse into barbarism." But before then the First World War broke out, and somehow civilization managed to survive it. Then came the League of Nations, based in part on Alfred Nobel's plan for "a convention under which all the governments would bind themselves to defend collectively any country that was attacked." Years of "uneasy peace" were interrupted by the Second World War. And then came the United Nations with its underlying principles of arbitration and mediation — more of Alfred Nobel's beliefs.

During all this time the Nobel peace prize has helped keep the cause of peace before the public. Of all the Nobel prizes it is the one which has attracted the most attention. People who associate dynamite with its wartime uses — with destruction rather than construction — are intrigued with the thought that the inventor of dynamite left part of his fortune for the promotion of peace. Some of them have even talked a lot of nonsense about Nobel's planning the peace prize as a sort of penance for having invented dynamite. Those persons do not realize that Nobel expected his invention to be used for industrial progress. They do not know of his lifelong hatred of war, his deep desire for peace.

People who put the peace prize apart from the other prizes and above them do not consider that in Nobel's mind science, literature, and peace all went hand in hand "in the wide field of knowledge and progress."

Perhaps they have not thought deeply about his belief that advancement in all these areas would win for mankind a wiser, saner, more peaceful world.

The atomic age and the hydrogen age have brought a reversion to Nobel's first and longest-held theory: that "the only thing that will ever prevent nations from beginning war is terror." We read of England's prime minister declaring that only the West's possession of nuclear weapons has prevented open aggression by the Soviet Union. Then we read the statement of one of America's great practical scientists, David Sarnoff, that the coming parity of deadly weapons, instead of acting as a restraining influence, may produce emotion which, "raised to a pitch of hysteria by the very magnitude of the menace, may vanquish reason."

But as the shadows lengthen we find some comfort in the thought that perhaps mankind, like Alfred Nobel, changes its thinking. Perhaps, like him, it may live through the "peace by terror" idea and come to believe that by continually advancing along all lines of knowledge, mankind will eventually win through to security and permanent peace. This, when he made his great and original gift to those who "have conferred the greatest benefit on mankind," was the belief of Alfred Nobel — inventor, scientist, and champion of peace.

SOURCE MATERIALS

Evlanoff, Michael. NOBEL — PRIZE DONOR (Blakiston-Revell, 1943)
Falnes, Oscar J. NORWAY AND THE NOBEL PEACE PRIZE (Columbia University, 1938)
Henriksson, Fritz. THE NOBEL PRIZES AND THEIR FOUNDER (Bonniers, Stockholm, 1938)
Kaplan, Flora, comp. NOBEL PRIZE WINNERS (Nobelle Publishing Company, Chicago, 1941)
MacCullum, Thomas W., and Taylor, Stephen. THE NOBEL PRIZE WINNERS AND THE NOBEL FOUNDATION (Central European Publishing Company, Zurich, 1938)
Pauli, Herta E. ALFRED NOBEL, DYNAMITE KING — ARCHITECT OF PEACE (Fischer, 1942)
Schück, H., Sohlman, R., et al., ed. by the Nobel Foundation. NOBEL, THE MAN AND HIS PRIZES (University of Oklahoma Press, 1951)
Sohlman, Ragnar, and Schück, Henrik. NOBEL, DYNAMITE AND PEACE (Cosmopolitan, 1929). Same material, though different arrangement, as THE LIFE OF ALFRED NOBEL (London, 1929)
Suttner, Bertha von. MEMOIRS (Ginn — for the International School of Peace — 1910)

Also pamphlets, including:
Armattoe, R. E. G. AWARD OF THE NOBEL PRIZES, DEC. 10, 1947 (privately printed)
Descany. LA FONDATION NOBEL (Academie Royale de Belgigue, Bulletin Ser. 3, 1900)
LES PRIX NOBEL EN 1901 (Imprimerie Royale, Stockholm, 1901 — on microfilm at New York Public Library)
Moe, R. LE PRIX NOBEL DE LA PAIX (Oslo, 1932)
Nauckhoff, John H. ALFRED NOBEL (In "Biographies of Scandinavians" file at American-Scandinavian library)

Also magazine articles, including:
Hedvall, Yngve. "Alfred Nobel, Inventor of Dynamite and Patron of Peace," *American-Scandinavian Review*, February, 1926

Landquist, John. "Alfred Nobel, Founder of the Nobel Prizes," *American-Scandinavian Review*, December, 1933

Lange, C. "The Future of the Norwegian Nobel Institute," *Independent*, 1907

Mosenthal, Henry de. "Alfred Nobel," *Nineteenth Century*, October, 1898

Spender, A. Edmund. "Alfred Nobel," *Westminster Review*, December, 1901

and other articles in magazines, including *Cosmopolitan, Forum, Living Age, Independent, Nation, Outlook, Saturday Review, Science News Letter, Scientific Digest, Scientific American, Science Monthly*, dating from 1898 to date.

INDEX

INDEX

INDEX

OIL. *See* Baku oil wells
Oil tankers, 153
Oscar II, of Sweden, 233, 234, 240, 269, 270, 272
Oslo. *See* Christiania

PANAMA CANAL COMPANY, 179-180
Paris, 27-28, 47, 90, 119-120, 124-126, 151, 220, 227-228, 235, 241, 242-243, 257-263; Nobel home in, 120, 121-123, 133-134, 170-171, 185-186, 214-215, 235, 241, 263, 271; laboratory in, 123-124, 129-130, 171, 182-183
Passy, Frédéric, 279
Patents. *See* Nobel, Alfred, patents
Peace. *See* Nobel, Alfred, peace ideas and actions; Nobel peace prize; Suttner, Bertha von
Pelouze, Théophile, 28
Portugal, dynamite factory in, 117
Prizes. *See* Nobel prizes
Prudhomme, Sully, 278
Pyroglycerin. *See* Nitroglycerin

RÖNTGEN, WILHELM KONRAD, 277
Rothschild family, 156-157
Royal Swedish Academy of Science. *See* Swedish Academy of Science
Russia, 5, 11, 25-26, 35, 41, 144, 177. *See also* Alexander II; Baku oil wells; Crimean War; Nicholas I; Russian Army; Russian Government; Russo-Turkish War; St. Petersburg
Russian Army, 20, 22-23, 51-52, 54, 68, 145
Russian Government, 40, 147, 156
Russo-Turkish War, 150, 151

ST. GOTTHARD TUNNEL, 131
St. Petersburg, Russia, 5, 12, 16-19, 23, 39, 48-50, 144-145, 158-159, 267
San Francisco, California, 96, 100, 103-104

INDEX

United States Blasting Oil Company, 105, 106, 107
Uppsala, University of, 11, 58, 211
VINTERVIKEN, SWEDEN, explosives factory, 84, 85, 87, 89, 91,
 145, 212
Waffen Nieder, Die, 192-193
War and peace. *See* Nobel, Alfred, peace ideas and actions
Wennerström, Herre, 83, 87
Will, Nobel's. *See* Nobel, Alfred, will
Winkler, Theodore, 91, 106
Winkler, W., 88-89

ZININ, PROF., 38, 51
Zurich, Switzerland, 198-203